EMBRACING 1

"Deepika Avanti takes us into the miraculous sacred worlds of the human body and, in doing so, she awakens us to our own sacred journey here on Mother Earth. In a vision I saw into the inner realms hundreds of titles yet to be published, and now I am thankful that *Embracing the Miraculous* is one of them."

Joseph Beautiful Painted Arrow

"Deepika's healing work is impeccable."

Kam Yuen, founder Chinese Energetics, Yuen Energetics

"From the many years I've known Deepika, I've been extremely impressed with her ability to heal herself from a life-threatening condition of Grave's disease and heal others from major illnesses. She has done all this from her connection to God. I deeply admire her connection and devotion to God. This is a powerful blessing that she successfully shares and inspires others to also live."

Ray Wynfield, Healer, Minister, Teacher of Meditation

"I have been waiting to really feel tangibly connected with God and supported to use this divine insight in every aspect of my life, including serving many businesses as a president and coach. This book and Deepika's work inspired me to succeed with God in ways I didn't imagine. You leap to new levels living this book."

Marilyn Laverty, President and Business Coach

"I'm so excited reading Deepika's personal stories that totally speak to me and inspire my life. Her simple exercises continually help me connect with God and heal on all levels. The results in my life are awesome and will be in yours too."

Julia Gibbs, a happily healed reader and client

"When you said, 'Do you feel God?,' I felt it. I now trust that whatever is going on is okay and for the best. I feel more peace in my life."

Marilyn Love

"We are here to connect with God, to go beyond ourselves and to experience the Great Mystery. Deepika has devoted her life to following her spiritual guides. She shares her personal experience along this path and wants nothing more than to inspire others to do the same."

Carlos Starr Ogsbury

"I had long-term problems with asthma, high blood pressure, heart, prostate, colon and skin problems. I had a cat scan showing my heart valve needed surgery. Three days after working with Deepika my heart was fine and the open heart surgery was not needed. Now I have low blood pressure, and the rest has basically cleared up too. I am breathing better than I have for years."

Jim, client

"I was diagnosed with Huntington's disease. Last year people couldn't understand me. Now I am able to have conversations and even understand scientific articles." [Brian went from an exhausted state, being in bed most of the time sleeping, to being totally active, even studying until midnight, walking a mile with his walker with no oxygen.]

Brian, client

"After seven long years of suffering from chronic fatigue syndrome and fibromyalgia, what a relief it was to find Deepika—a true healer whose heart, hands, and combined healing talents brought me to a new level of health and well being."

Claire, client

"Deepika's wisdom runs as deep as the compassion in her heart, for all beings, everywhere. She has answered her soul's challenge to become fully awakened in this lifetime, and to live in moment-to-moment connection with Divinity. Her devotion and great facility in helping each of us to discover our own highest and healed self are a wondrous miracle, here to open and bloom in the light of your present reality."

m. Claire, author, healer, presenter, teacher

"Imagine a world where All of us experience Infinite Love within ourselves, with each other, and we live Namaste, which means, I bow to the God within you. Deepika's book ignites this reality, bringing it alive within us. We invite you to join this mission of living love on earth."

Steve Farrell, Worldwide Coordinating Director, Humanity's Team (in 97 countries), info@humanitysteam.org

EMBRACING
THE
MIRACULOUS

Attaining Optimal Health
on All Levels

DEEPIKA AVANTI

BLUE DOLPHIN PUBLISHING

Published by Blue Dolphin Publishing, Inc.
P.O. Box 8, Nevada City, CA 95959
Orders: 1-800-643-0765
Web: www.bluedolphinpublishing.com

ISBN: 978-1-57733-211-4

Library of Congress Cataloging-in-Publication Data

Avanti, Deepika.
   Embracing the miraculous : attaining optimal health on
all levels / Deepika Avanti.
        p. cm.
   Includes bibliographical references.
   ISBN 978-1-57733-211-4 (pbk. : alk. paper)
   1. Mental healing. 2. Spiritual healing. I. Title.

RZ400.A93 2008
615.8'51—dc22

                                        2007044215

First printing: March, 2008

Printed in the United States of America

10   9   8   7   6   5   4   3   2   1

dedicated to
all of us feeling divinely loved,
sensing universal energy,
knowing we are one with the Miraculous, God by all names,
attaining Optimal Health,
physically, mentally, emotionally, spiritually,
all of us blessing all existence with love

Contents

John of God and Deepika

Acknowledgments

I'd like to thank everyone whose help and inspirations created this book. I thank John of God, and the Spirits of Light who gave me this book. I thank everyone at the Casa de Don Ignacio, whose love inspired me to share these experiences worldwide.

I thank Paul Clemens and the staff at Blue Dolphin for being an ideal publisher, and for all their guidance and friendship beyond my wildest dreams. My editor, Jasmin Cori, jasmin@jasmincori.com, thank you for your ongoing commitment, long hours and love. I thank my book cover designer, Robert Piller, robertpiller@yahoo.com, who created instant magic from my photos and dream.

I am so grateful to all my friends, colleagues, teachers, clients, and students, authors and speakers for your contributions, endorsements, support and time sharing incredible conversations with me. Thanks Jill Jones, Marilyn Laverty, Julia Gibbs, Ray Wynfield, Danae Shanti, Linda Lee, Marilyn Love, Claudia Medina, Harv Ecker, Kam Yuen, Joseph Rael, Osho, Vianna Stibel, teachers at Naropa University. Thanks, thanks, thanks.

I thank my soul-mate Charles Ogsbury and our son, Zen Ogsbury, for your dearest love, intimacy, nurturing, humor and support, which gave me time and energy to write. I thank my parents, Gene and George, and my family, Michelle, Diane, Jeff, Randy, and Peggy, for your love and first lessons in life teaching me about healing work.

Last but not least, I thank God for using my life in this way, and my dogs, the earth and the sun for helping me to be a clear medium for the book to flow through.

Introduction

Why do you want to Embrace the Miraculous? What is the Miraculous anyway? The Miraculous is Universal Energy. My life passion has been learning to trust this Miraculous Energy.

About ten years ago I went from being exhausted, unable to walk, barely alive, to now climbing 21,000 foot glacier peaks! Ah Ho!

Is there a health issue or life situation that seems impossible for you to change?

How would you like to know how to change your impossible situation and have the type of change I experienced? This book shares my stories of "impossible situations," how I embraced this Miraculous Universal Energy, gained optimal health on all levels, and also shows you how to change *your* "impossible" situations.

How would you like to have more Universal Energy to have better relationships: with yourself physically? emotionally? mentally? and spiritually? How about having more energy to have better relationships with your family? friends? career? home? and/or money? How about having more energy to serve and benefit the world? Did you answer "Yes" to any of these? Then this book will help you.

This book is based on my own efforts to gain optimal health and on my holistic healing practice, in which many clients have gotten their lives back, as well as classes I was given by Spirit to help all of us connect more deeply with this

Universal Energy. How would you like to develop a deeper trust in God, by any name you choose, by tangibly sensing, feeling, hearing, seeing and being moved by the Universal Energy? *Embracing the Miraculous* has over forty exercises that teach you how to be one with the Miraculous, Divine Love that you are, and attain optimal health on all levels. How would you like to attain optimal health or have better health?

The Course in Miracles describes miracles as a change of perception from the ego or lower self to the (Big) Self. This book gives you body-centered experiences to change your perception from the ego to God's perception. By changing your inner world, your outer world changes. If everyone had God perception, we would have a world based on love.

The book is divided into two parts. The first helps you have a more tangible experience of God and learn to follow guidance. The second half centers on achieving optimal health through becoming aware of limiting beliefs, creating positive beliefs, healing emotional wounds, gaining more peace and joy, considering tools that support the body in healing, and learning how to use meditation to deepen your relationship with Spirit and live each moment in the present. My wish is for you to have this connection with Divine Love and the optimal health on all levels that comes with it. What my life so clearly shows is that all is possible when Embracing the Miraculous.

Part I
Embracing the Miraculous

I

Dancing with Spirit

*"Your first responsibility is to your spiritual side.... Create an
inner harmony where your loving soul guides your physical
behavior, rather than having your soul coming in second place,
following physical outbursts."*
—Wayne Dyer, *Real Magic*, p. 104

*How would your like to have more energy
to live your potential?*

Tricked into God

How do you embrace Universal Energy, the Miraculous,
God by infinite names, to attain optimal health? How do
you physically heal from being 95% dead to climbing 21,000-
foot mountain peaks? How do you emotionally heal terror
and depression? How do you mentally heal deep beliefs
of being unloved and unwanted? How do you spiritually
heal and learn to trust God? How do you advance—from
surrendering to God and God's Will in only life-and-death
or tantalizing situations—to living a life devoted to God and
feeling divinely loved and connected to the Miraculous each
moment all day long? How do you go from not trusting God
to knowing you are one with God?

Most of us just want more physical energy to get more
out of life and this spiritual idea of God can wait for tomorrow. I was told tomorrow might would not be happening by
doctors looking at my blood tests. God was done waiting.

What I discovered is that our relationship with God is the source of all our energy. If we want more physical energy, the way to get it the quickest is reconnecting spiritually. This is what saved my life. If I had gone after the physical solution I would be dead right now. If you are convinced that the physical solution needs to be first and God can wait please turn to the second half of this book. However, if you really want more energy, continue reading about how to tap into the Universal Source of infinite energy. This energy for me is like opening to 550 volts, or opening up to a mini lightning strike that never stops. Do you want an extra 220 volts coming to you? Read on.

Sometimes I wondered if my life was one of God's cosmic jokes. As a spirit, I saw sad, scared people on earth. I wanted to wake everyone up to their essence of Divine Love and their oneness with God. I agreed to this mission, rejoicing at how easy it would be. But God tricked me. I spent the next fifty years fearfully resisting God, while also yearning to find God. I was born living in the same boat feeling sad and scared.

My life in the womb began with nearly dying, suffocating from smoke, and starving. In the incubator, I felt frozen and abandoned, afraid of disappearing into nothingness. The finale of my first year was being thrown against a wall at eight months old. (You can guess what beliefs molded the rest of my life. Subconscious fears of being afraid of dying and being hurt ran my life, as well as beliefs that I am not wanted, not loved, not cared about, and I must not be good enough.) I decided to hide out as a cat meowing under chairs for the next four years, as I was too terrified to speak to my mother. I trusted no one, especially not God. The only times I prayed while growing up was when I was facing death. Then I felt helpless, with nowhere else to turn, out of desperation beseeching God to help me.

I didn't understand how this battle for and against God served my (unconscious) higher purpose until I was flattened and ninety-five percent dead with what the doctors consider an "incurable disease" (hyperthyroidism). My guidance said five words over and over to me: "Don't radiate. You will heal." For three years, I didn't undergo the radiation treatment that the doctors saw as so necessary, and I didn't heal. Three doctors gave me the death verdict; the last one gave me three weeks to live. Was I going to trust the voices of these external doctors or God's voice within? Was I going to live or die?

When I was sick and dying, I had the insight that my healing would come from becoming one with Spirit. I had spent my entire life seeking this and obviously had not succeeded. Now I had no choice but to succeed. I committed to trusting and following guidance out of my deep desire to avoid death. In the process, I did much, much more than simply avoid dying. I learned to "live love by living God."

Spiritual Healing Comes First

When we decide to heal spiritually, we must understand that what our ego or personality wants is usually not the same goal that Spirit knows is best for us. We need to learn to trust the process. The process may seem like it is not giving our ego what it wants, when it wants it, and this is probably true. Our egos are like two-year-olds demanding, "I want this, and I want it now!" and Spirit is like a wise parent who tells the child, "There is something better for you that I will give you, but you will have to wait for the secret to be revealed."

When I was so sick, unable to walk, exhausted and trembling, I read something that inspired me. It invited me to compare my sick self to a vision of my well self. I asked my well self how it became well, what it had learned that was different from how my sick self was operating.

My well body said it had learned to be one with Spirit. My first response was to try to bargain with Spirit. "Heal my physical body, then I will know how to be one with Spirit and will give my life to Spirit."

I was shocked at the response. The words appeared to me visually. I was told in no uncertain terms that *I needed to be one with Spirit first* for healing to happen. I had it backwards.

I was frustrated that Spirit wouldn't bargain with me. I just wanted my physical body back. I was also scared; I didn't know how to be one with Spirit. That was the problem. How was I suppose to do what I did not know how to do? How do I, a tangible, finite physical being become one with that which seems intangible, undefinable, and infinite?

Being faced with death speeds things up. I decided that I had to trust this guidance and commit to following guidance all day every day in an attempt to be one with this "unknown" Spirit. I didn't know Christ or God, but I believed there was an overall energetic harmony of love that was greater than myself. (I had been a practicing Buddhist and worked for years in the Shamanic field.) I hoped that my attempt to follow guidance would bring me closer to being one with Spirit and that I would heal. I could only proceed on hope, belief, and faith. It took years for me to know God by all names.

I now understand that my quickly regaining optimal health wasn't Spirit's most important goal for me. Spirit's goal was my learning the *process* of being one with God, one with the Miraculous.

John of God

I have been helped tremendously in my journey of becoming one with God by a Brazilian man known as John of God, whose given name is Joao Teixera de Faria (born in 1942). He has helped millions of people heal through the volunteer work he does as a medium channeling elevated spirits at the Casa de Dom Ignacio in Abadiana, Brazil. (In future references, I'll simply use "the Casa" to refer to this center.)

Daily, he says the prayer, "Master, do as Thou whilst with my body," and surrenders totally. His soul leaves, he loses conscious awareness of himself as the contemporary Brazilian man he is, and an elevated soul of infinite love uses his body for about six or more hours a day providing healing for the thousands of people in line who simply walk past him. The energy of Christ's love comes through about thirty-eight different spirits, including doctors who have passed to the other side. When he is in trance, working this way, no matter which of the particular spirits is operating through him, it is simply referred to as "the Entity." Over fourteen million people have received healings in addition to all the healings going out to relatives and friends of those who come to see him.

I barely know the man, Joao, but he is a model for me of surrender, love of God, and service, and the Entity(ies) has become my master teacher in life. My experience of the Entity(ies) is of Christ, being in the presence of infinite love, understanding, wisdom, power, and healing. Christ is my spiritual teacher now and manifests on earth to me as the Entity(ies). I have grown to treasure and love Christ and the Entity(ies) with all my being, my heart, soul, and mind.

My life and every aspect is devoted to loving God, Christ, the Entity(ies), all of which I experience as Divine Love—and to following Thy Will. It was my experience of connecting with these Entities, these Spirits of Light, sensing their presence, feeling loved, seeing, hearing, being physically moved, and intuiting them that created my love affair. Feeling Christ's love, stronger than any earthly love I've ever felt, tricked me into devoting my life to God.

I was lucky to have Joao, a physical human being, chan-neling the Entity(ies) or Christ essence, because I needed an earthly experience of God in order to continue falling in love with the Divine and to surrender so completely. The Entities who use Joao's body became my *Beloved*, just as Ram Dass experienced his guru Maharaji as *Beloved*. Spirit was too nebulous for me to devote my life to at first.

Ram Dass felt the same connection energetically with his guru all the time, so when his guru left his body, there was no difference for Ram Dass. After several visits, my awareness grew, and I was able to feel this connection with the Entities and Christ all the time. More and more, I was experiencing God as light and love within myself. Within a year there was nothing more important to me than loving God, personal-ized as the Entity(ies), Christ and other people. Now a year and a half later, all I do has become a prayer of love to serve God.

I use to wonder how Ram Dass could be so in love with his guru. I thought that to love a guru was a sign of weak-ness. I had no idea how much courage it takes. I also didn't realize that it would elicit an adoration and love I had never experienced before. I never knew I would experience the infinite love of Christ in a teacher on earth. My heart is filled almost every moment, and my eyes are misty with tears of gratitude and adoration for the Entity(ies).

One day Joao was on stage, hardly able to speak, with tears rolling down his cheeks as he talked about how grate-ful he was for the Entities being in his life. I had never felt anyone's heart as big as this. I wondered how anyone could love such a nebulous unknown (as Spirit) so much. It wasn't until I experienced this relationship with the Entity(ies) of Light myself that I understood the love and gratitude Joao expressed that day.

On his birthday, he served an estimated 10,000 visitors at the Casa in his trance state, doing healings as the Entity from

8 a.m. until 6 p.m. with a two-hour lunch break. How many clients do I see a day, I pondered, or the busiest doctor or hospital? My head spins. Just looking at 1,000 people would be overwhelming, without also scanning all of them and doing healings on them. Then Joao proceeded to serve 10,000 people from what appeared to be a birthday cake that was a block long, the biggest cake I'd ever seen in my life. (It was actually thousands of cakes put together as one cake.) I stood astounded. I looked at him across a hundred people; he met my eyes and continued to gaze at me until I was saturated with his message (in action) that life was about service.

You would never have caught me working on my birthday! This was the day I insisted that my husband and son serve me. I think somewhere I had missed the boat, big time. God, why didn't you give me an instruction manual? At age 52, I was finding out this life isn't about all the physical things I had prioritized.

I had been taught to be successful, but what was success? For a long time, I thought it was completing my goals. Then it was living in joy and love. So I worked to complete my goals concerning health, growth, my child, husband, house, finances, career, friends, other business goals, and so forth with love and joy. These goals had replaced God as priority, and my motivation was to gain some sort of external success, appreciation, fame, and reward.

Living Thy Will confused me. What I had judged as important wasn't what Thy Will was guiding me to do. I no longer had my list of goals. I didn't know what was going to happen. My full-time job became connecting with and following the Miraculous within myself. My motivation became loving God within, and success was now defined in terms of my relationship with God. Each morning meditation I connect and ask to do Thy Will, as well as with each decision throughout the day. A rush of energy with a voice and picture guides me. When my ego gets upset, I remind myself that I am on an eternal spiritual journey realizing my oneness with God. All I need to do is love, trust, and follow God. I thank John of God for his role model.

Lessons from Peace Pilgrim

Have any of you seen the film or book about "Peace Pilgrim"? She is such a shining example of living and following Spirit, putting her life on the line every moment of every day. Naturally, it took her a number of years to come to this depth of surrender. Once she decided, she left behind all her belongings except for her *Peace Pilgrim* shirt, a comb in her pocket, a pair of pants, and shoes. For twenty-eight years, she walked over 25,000 miles on a personal pilgrimage for peace. She trusted that she would be given the shelter, food, and water that she needed. How many of us surrender to Spirit, trusting at this depth?

Her experience of peace involved relinquishing the ego and becoming one with universal consciousness. Peace Pilgrim describes how, once she found that place, it was like being able to return to a mountain top more often and for longer periods of time. In this state of oneness, she had total confidence that all problems already had a solution. This allowed her to sustain a state of peace. I really admire her. (For more information, see www.PeacePilgrim.com.)

I think the scary part is letting go, being vulnerable, receptive, and trusting the so-called "unknown." Somehow, living from ego had made me feel more in control of my life, stronger, more like I knew what was going to happen. I laugh as I write about this illusion my ego created, thinking that life is known.

Thy Will Is My Will

I tried something similar to Peace Pilgrim, committing to following *Thy will is my will* and going into the unknown. (I will use the phrase "Thy Will" to refer to this.) I am living in total spontaneity, following guidance, not knowing one minute to the next what Spirit will have me do. My only goal is being open, in love, connected to Spirit, and following guidance.

At first it was scary living this way. Living Thy Will makes me feel less in control and more vulnerable. But the reality I found in living surrendered to Spirit also makes me feel more loved, safe, and protected, because this Divine Love presence is always vibrating within me. Ultimately my life is alive with more love and joy, and I am doing things that are bringing out the best in me, benefiting more people than before.

All I have to do is ask, "Thy will is my will; what do I do? What is your perspective? What is the question I need to ask you to get the right answer?"

What I am told is often challenging, new, and not what my personality feels comfortable doing. But many times, by following the Miraculous a magical situation manifests in which I feel totally blessed and supported. Here is an example.

I was in Peru high in the mountains traveling with a small group, including several guides. One day I was photographing a bright red flower. I thought that I was there for a few minutes, but I must have been engrossed for longer. Thirty burros and nine people disappeared from sight with no footprints or trail to follow. The burros had all my equipment, except for one extra shirt.

I panicked. "Spirit, move my body where I am to go," I prayed. My body started moving toward some rocky cliffs, but I couldn't see any route a burro could navigate. I panicked again. "Spirit, help me." It seemed like hours had gone by. All I knew was that camp was eight miles from where I was, and I didn't even have a coat. I knelt down. "Help me, Spirit."

A bright red and yellow bird appeared three feet in front of me. It flew twenty feet and stopped, as if waiting for me. I followed it. For the next hour, I followed the bird, climbing the cliffs to the top of a ridge 1000 feet up. At the top of the ridge was a dirt trail in which I could see peoples' tracks. I ran the next seven miles and found camp at sunset. That bird saved my life. A month later, it was outside my bedroom window in Colorado one morning. It was a tropical bird that I had never seen before and haven't seen since. A manifestation of the Miraculous.

How My Life Has Changed

My life has grown so much in just one year of devoting myself to the Miraculous and practicing *Thy will is my will*. I used to feel a lot of background anxiety. Many people who have been abused tend toward worry and hyper-vigilance. We are always on the lookout to prevent being hurt. After developing this connection with Divine Love, I often have silence, pure light, and a flood of comforting energy as my companion. I am able to "relax" (this word did not exist in my vocabulary a year ago) and can tune in any time I wish to meditate and receive guidance.

Before this, I was like so many Americans, using my daily planner to create a life; now my life is planned by the Miraculous, ever so much more artfully and spontaneously. I lived for the goals that my ego created, until Spirit stopped me in my tracks several times.

For example, I used to dream of being a successful, famous artist, until all my galleries closed the same week. What was going on? In a vision quest, I was shown a picture of how my life would be if I followed my ego. I saw myself selling my art but dying with a sad heart. I saw another option of being used as a healer, taking advantage of the channeling skills I had learned as an artist. I saw that my heart would be fulfilled at my death if I followed Spirit's path for me. This is the path that I chose.

Now I decide with Spirit, and I devote my life to having all my actions love and serve God. Rather than strive for the world's definition of success, I am now motivated by what I have defined as success, which is connecting with the Miraculous.

My mind, which used to be in a state of constant worry, is focused now on the Miraculous within and on feeling my heart. I am more present than I've ever been, and I notice the beauty all around me. If worry arises, Spirit reassures me and loves me all the more, gently coaxing me to continue. I may express my fears, anger, or sadness about following guidance; then Spirit consoles me and reminds me what is really important. My daily planner gets filled in guided by Spirit rather than my logical mind. My comfort zones aren't Spirit's priority. It is my love and devotion and knowing this God perspective knows best that keeps me going into the unknown, following Thy Will.

I have challenges, but I experience my soul and the universe conspiring to support me to grow more unconditionally loving in every way, evolving me into the Divine Love that I really am. Life's challenges are meaningful lessons that nudge me into examining my emotions and subconscious beliefs so that I may heal more deeply. I feel more relaxed and comfortable knowing that the Miraculous is guiding me, regardless of how challenging the situation is. I know Divine Love loves me more than I have ever known. Wherever I am, guidance is on purpose, even if I don't know what this purpose is.

Being Danced by Divine Love

I can't tell you how happy and utterly grateful I've become since I decided to risk surrendering to Divine Love. Now there is nothing I desire beyond this surrendering. There is nothing more my heart wants than to be devoted to Divine Love and for my soul to be one with the highest love and wisdom. I am so grateful to sense this Divine Love talking into my ear as my best friend. I am so grateful to be spoken through, written through, and moved through.

Over time, I have learned to love, not because of what Spirit has done for me, but because of my connection with Spirit. We are love; we are one, intermingled in love. It is a love that fills me and "dances" my life. I embrace God, and God embraces me.

2

Opening to Divine Love

There is so much love available, it is as abundant as the air you breathe (p. 93).

—*Living with Joy: Keys to Personal Power
Spiritual Transformation*, Sanaya Roman

How would you like to open to more Divine Love?

Becoming one with Spirit starts with getting acquainted. I had previously thought that getting acquainted with Spirit was impossible, because Spirit was too nebulous. But through my journey, I have learned that we can feel, touch, see, taste, and hear Spirit, just as we can a person.

In this chapter we'll look at some basic foundations for developing this relationship and use some active explorations for you to begin this process. You can also hear the next eleven explorations with beautiful music by ordering my DVD or by taking my classes (see back of book).

Becoming Still

To get acquainted with Divine Love, it is necessary to become meditative and receptive by going inside, slowing down, and becoming aware of subtle physical sensations, emotions (fear, anger, sadness, happiness or love), thoughts, and spiritual inspiration.

My biggest pitfall (as I see it now) was not becoming still, inward, aware, and silent. *Peace* and *relaxation* were foreign words to my Puritan fixation on "doing." Meditation was a real key for me, although it wasn't until I got into the mantra meditations and feeling the love of Spirit during meditation that I really enjoyed it. (I had "meditated" for thirty years at this point.) It was not until I started living from a state of *being*, rather than my habitual *doing*, that my life really changed. I became more peaceful.

The qualities of being present, peaceful, open, and aware are important aspects of receiving. You can assist in this by creating a time that does not have to be hurried or interrupted. You want to become open to allowing an experience of the unknown to flow through you. I know people who think that angels don't exist—and they won't exist for those people who have already made up their mind. You have to temporarily suspend your judgments so that you can be receptive.

My second pitfall was not being patient and not knowing to watch for subtle shifts. I was looking for a thunderbolt to strike me dead like episodes in the *Bible*, and when this didn't happen, I gave up. I am sure my requests were answered, but I was too busy to notice something as subtle as a slight sensation of something like a breeze come through my body. So if you have been impatient or just unaware, try doing the following exercises and explorations after you have exercised or worked hard, and are willing to just be present, inwardly directed, peaceful, open, receptive, and patient, with alert awareness.

My third pitfall was editing my experience after I received it. I am sure that I probably saw Christ, because now I do in meditation and healing work. But back then I must have pushed the delete button and negated the experience, thinking that I made it up.

Allow your experience to unfold, trusting that what happens is valid, "good enough," and "right." In fact, it is perfect! Negatively judging the experience or yourself only closes you off from being open to Divine Love. Trust that all the experiences that you have which are prompted by the instructions in this book are special and valuable—and so they will be.

It is also important to put your body in a relaxed state. You might use progressive relaxation to accomplish this. Here is a basic relaxation exercise you can do to precede any exercise in the book. This and the other exercises in the first half of the book are included on the *Embracing the Miraculous* CD (order at the back of this book).

Master Relaxation Exercise

Find a comfortable place where you will not be disturbed for fifteen to thirty minutes. Drink some water and put a paper and pen by your side for easy access so that you can integrate your experience afterwards if you want. Sit or lie down (if you can stay awake) with your arms and legs uncrossed so the energy can flow best. Shut your eyes. Feel your back against the surface it is resting upon. Feel yourself getting heavier as you sink into this support.

Then tighten all the muscles in your entire body. Take in a deep breath and hold for a count of 1000, 2000, 3000. When you are ready, release your breath. Repeat this two more times, tightening your entire body and releasing.

Now scan your body from head to foot, checking to see if all of your muscles are relaxed. Tune into your head, eyes, forehead, cheeks, jaw, ears, and neck. Are all these muscles relaxed? If not, simply tighten the area, hold, and release, repeating until the area relaxes. Continue with your shoulders, upper back, and chest. Tighten (if needed) and relax. Check your upper arms, lower arms, hands, and fingers. Relax this area. Check your diaphragm, abdomen, middle back, and lower back. Tighten (if needed) and release. Check your buttocks and genitals; tighten and relax. Check your upper and lower legs, feet and toes; tighten and relax.

Now quickly scan your entire body again for any tightness. Where there is tension, tighten and relax. This entire process can take ten minutes or less than one minute after you get good at it.

Now imagine that you are walking into an elevator. Push the button to go down seven stories (65 feet), which is the receptive theta state where healing more easily occurs. Feel your body dropping as you count down *seven, six,* getting heavier, getting deeper. *Five, four,* deepening and dropping even more. *Three, two,* feel yourself totally relaxed and very, very deep. *One,* feel yourself one with spirit in a deeply relaxed state.

To come out of this state, say, "I am feeling light and invigorated throughout my entire body." Feel you back rest against the surface behind you. Feel your entire body head to toes, then wiggle your entire body taking several deep breaths.

Open your eyes and notice details in the room all around you. Take a drink of water. Stand up and shuffle your feet across the floor, feeling heaviness in your feet grounding you to the earth.

Look in a mirror and see yourself as an adult person. Then integrate the exercise by writing in a journal, if you wish.

Using the Body as a Barometer

You can use the body as an instrument to reflect to you how specific words affect you. You should be able to feel your breath change from deeper to more shallow, sense areas of your body tightening or relaxing, notice emotions such as sadness, fear, or anger, and be aware of negative thoughts.

Here is an exercise to play with.

1. Notice your body sensations, your breath, your emotions, and your thoughts when you say to yourself in a mirror, "I love you." What happens?
2. Now sense your body and say to yourself in the mirror, "You're not good enough." What emotions, sensations, and thoughts happen?
3. Now check in with your body and notice what happens when I ask, "Are you open to sensing divinity in your body?" Notice subtleties of body sensations; check your stomach and neck, and look to see if any areas tightened up. What happens emotionally? Is there happiness? fear?

The Power of Names

Words are powerful and have a large impact on our bodies, which becomes more apparent when we are aware of what is happening inside of us. Since words are so important, we can use this same process to identify the most powerful word for the Divine for you.

Exploration: Name the Divine

1. Repeat the relaxation procedure introduced above or any other that you are comfortable with. Then say, "God loves me," and see how that feels.
2. Now substitute the words Spirit, Universal Energy, Source of all energy, Divine Love, Higher Power, Light, Cosmic Consciousness, the Miraculous, or Allah. You might also work with messengers of God such as Christ, Mary, Buddha, Mohammad, and angels or other teachers.
3. Now come up with some words of your own. Sense your breath, your body's expansion and contraction, your

level of relaxation or tightness, your emotions, and your thoughts with each word.

The word you pick is important. The most powerful word for you may be a word that initially has a lot of negative connotations. As an example, I couldn't say the word *God* without feeling sick to my stomach until I was fifty years old. This came from my association of this word with being forced, when growing up, to go to the Mormon Church in Salt Lake City, Utah. My parents weren't Mormon, but wanted me to know about the Mormon culture. Since my parents drank coffee, Jack Daniels, and smoked, I was asked to sit separately in a corner of the room at the Mormon Sunday school. After twelve years of this, I would get sick to my stomach and vomit when I heard the word *God*. *Christ* was no better. I used the word *Spirit* for years, but found that it was not as inclusive for me as the word *God*, so I had to heal my issues around *God* and *Christ* to use these names. So keep in mind that your word may change.

4. Now look at the words that had the most negative associations for you. Take a few minutes to look for negative associations. Imagine putting these negative associations in the incinerator or into the sun and burning them up (use the trash method in "Clearing the Way" below). What is the impact on your body now when you say this word? Which is the most powerful, loving word for you now?

Clearing the Way

Our beliefs definitely limit our experience. Let's look at some of your beliefs as they relate to your experience with the Divine. When you find beliefs that you don't wish to have any more, delete or trash them using Chinese Energetics (www.yuenmethod.com) that Dr. Kam Yuen developed and

I teach). Your trash can be a black hole, the earth, the sun, or an incinerator—whatever feels complete in its elimination. When you trash a belief, connect it to your God level, Higher Source, mind, brain, spinal cord, body, system, organ tissue, cell, molecule, atom, quantum particle to the minus infinite 100% potential. Release all memories, imprints, residues on the physical, mental, emotional, psychological, psychic, spiritual, unconscious, conscious, and genetic levels. Use this technique when I say trash it in any of the exercises.

Exercise

- Sense your body. Have you ever been told that you couldn't directly sense God and there had to be an intermediary like a priest, saint, or prophet? If so, trash this. Now sense you body again. Notice the change.
- Sense your body. Were you told the energy of God would overpower you? Trash this. Notice the change in your body.
- Do you feel that you deserve this connection and experience? Do you feel able to have this connection? Search for any blocks, sense your body, and put these in the trash. Notice the change within.
- Do you feel willing to experience God as a sensation inside your body? Is only the Pope qualified, or priests, or men? Who deserves to have this experience more than you? Trash any limiting beliefs and sense the change.
- Do you feel you need to earn the right to this experience? Do you feel that it needs to take a certain number of years to gain access to sensing God? Ask yourself if there are any other blocks or beliefs that keep you from sensing God now. If so, dump them in the trash.
- Does sensing and connecting with God mean too much responsibility? Trash this. How does your body feel now compared to when we began this exercise? Different, right?

Using Prayer to Enhance Your Connection to God
(by any name)

Prayer is a powerful way to enhance our connection with God. When we pray, we are opening ourselves to Divine Love, to God, and magnifying the energy. This is especially important when you are trying to sense God. Before an exploration, I recommend you say a prayer to make your experience more powerful.

This is my daily prayer that you may use also:

Thy Will is My Will, God. Each day, use my thoughts as your thoughts, God; use my eyes to see your love and beauty, God; use my ears to hear you; use my voice to speak your thoughts, God; place my heart in your heart to expand your love, God; use my intuition to be guided by you; use my entire body, my life, my time, my money, use all of me and all I have for the highest love, joy, and purpose. Use me to live Christ Consciousness and Love. Use me to love and serve you in every way, God.

Here is a prayer you might play with to help get more acquainted with divinity.

I ask Divine Love (or Mother/Father God by all names, Christ, the Entities, the Miraculous, angels, guides, or whatever name you choose) to assist me and magnify my experience so your presence is definitely known and felt. Thank you (name) for your heightened presence.

Imagining the Reality You Want

Another important technique for supporting change is imagining the reality you want. This imagining has to be done as fully and completely as possible, so you really know it through all your being. This, in essence, prepares you for the experience and makes it more likely.

Exercise

- Feel your life right now. How is it? Now imagine your life with a constant sensation of Divine Love/God in your body.
- Imagine feeling Divine Love always with you. Imagine speaking with Divine Love more easily and having answers come quickly. Imagine knowing beyond a doubt that you sense and feel Divine Love within your body. Now how do you imagine your life being different?
- Do you want this life with Divine Love/God that you are imagining?
- Is your answer yes? If so, in Chapter 3 we'll be getting acquainted with this love.
- Is your answer 100% yes? It is normal to not feel 100% committed. There are fears about taking on this responsibility, fears of the unknown, fears about following Thy Will. Many of these will be addressed later in the book. It is essential to work through these obstacles if you want to develop this relationship.

God wants to put a new song in your heart. He wants to fill you with hope. He wants you to know that He loves you more than you can imagine (p. 70).... He always accepts you. He always confirms you value.... You will always be the apple of His eye. He will never give up on you....
— *Your Best Life Now: 7 Steps to Living at Your Full Potential*, Joel Osteen

Let's move now, to getting acquainted.

3

Getting Acquainted with Divine Love

Our goal is God. Nothing short of that goal will bring us joy (p. 248). The endless chain of communication between loved and lover, between God and man, is the most beautiful song, the sweetest poem. It is the highest art and the most passionate love (p. 259).

—Marianne Williamson, *A Return to Love: Reflections on the Principles of* A Course in Miracles

How would you like to feel more Divine Love?

Once you have opened yourself to Divine Love (God by any name), you are ready to start having actual experiences of the Miraculous.

Sensing Where Your Soul and God Join (Within Your Body)

God connects with our soul, though often we are unaware of this Divine Love connection. Our soul is the conscious memory and Divine Love energy that continues as our spirit after the death of our body. Here is an exercise that may help you to feel this.

- Imagine that you feel your soul in your heart area.

24

- Put on some loving music and call in God, the angels, and guides as you ask to sense and feel God in your soul. Give yourself twenty minutes to sense and feel God saturating your soul with love and joining your heart with the deepest love and adoration you have ever felt. See and feel heaven as the Divine Love of your soul embracing and supporting your heart, just like heaven embracing the earth. This is often a deep experience moving people to tears as their hearts and souls open to God. It is a marriage between heaven and our earth body.

The Downward (Heaven-to-Earth) Flow of God (Masculine)

When you ask God to flow through you, often you will feel a subtle rush of energy, like a wind blowing through your body. I feel it as a downward flow of energy with a lot of strength in it and which is very grounding, yet which makes me feel light. It is as if I am a rod of light connecting heaven to earth like a magnet of energy. Many people feel it as a calm, warming waterfall flowing down their body. It is stable, consistent, and comforting.

This downward flow of energy, heaven-to-earth, is considered the masculine aspect. (This assumes you associate heaven with above, which is what most people do.)

Exercise

1. Begin with a prayer asking (your name for) God to heighten your sensations and awareness to feel this flow of universal energy and to magnify this flow so you feel it without a doubt. Give yourself another twenty minutes to sense the universal energy of God, like a waterfall falling from the heavens into your head. Feel this presence coming into your head, as a kind of thickening, dense

sensation. This sensation can be very subtle. When you can feel it in your head, then feel it come down your throat, through your shoulders, chest, abdomen, hips, thighs, lower legs, and feet into the center of the earth. Experiment to know if you feel this universal energy best standing up or sitting down. Again, call in God, the angels, and guides to magnify this energy so that you may feel it more strongly. As the energy comes down, the energy may hit pockets of stagnation. Be patient. Sense it and continue to call on God to help you feel the flow of energy more. This may take a lot of practice. You may feel it in your head but not any further. Don't give up. Keep practicing.

2. Focus on this universal energy flowing like a waterfall or shower, hitting the top of your head and flowing down through your body to the center of the earth. You can add light to this sensation and visualize the sun flowing downward with the water. If you want the sensation to be stronger, imagine the water magnetically drawing you downward. You may try holding a crystal. (Be aware that some crystals draw energy down, while others draw upward.) Once you feel this for even a second, you can repeat it, so allow yourself to be aware of this flow coming down through your body now.

When you sense God in your body, what happens to you? How does this change your life? This may not be something you can answer immediately. You can explore this relationship for the next week, month, or year. For me, being able to sense God answered a fifty-year question about God existing and my being part of God. I asked the Entity to help me have the awareness of this universal flow of love connecting through my body all of the time. You can ask God for the same request. Now I feel blessed with this connection and awareness. I feel it as a (gentle) magnetic lightning rod of flowing energy, loving and calming me all of the time. Reinforcing this universal energy to run down through your body rejuvenates you and keeps you younger.

Here is an advanced exercise that helps to balance the chakras. When you get good at sensing the flow of the masculine universal energy moving from heaven to earth, you can do this variation.

Exercise: Balancing Chakras with the Flow of God

- Imagine the sun or sunlight going from heaven down through your body to the center of the earth and then back up to your heart. Imagine this sunlight going out in all directions from your body—from the front, sides, and back. See if you can feel it going fifteen feet beyond your body and then if you can increase it to thirty feet. Keep increasing until it goes all the way around the earth. This helps to balance the positive and negative, masculine and feminine polarities in your body. Cosme Castanieto gave a similar version of this to me saying it was the Filipino shortcut to realign and balance all your chakras. This energy also rejuvenates you. Do it several times a day.

Exercise: Experiencing the Masculine Aspect of God

- Be open to seeing God in any form. In the book, *Extraordinary Times, Extraordinary Beings*, Wayne Peterson describes seeing Christ (or Maitreya) as a bike rider wearing spandex. You just never know! God is infinite and there are infinite ways to visualize God.
- Imagine yourself in a theta state (by going up or down sixty-five feet). This allows you to open to the spiritual realm in a more meditative state.
- Travel through the heavens to where you are able to meet the essence of God. This can be a place in heaven

or heaven within your heart. Visualize the surroundings and see God. Sense God's presence. How do you feel emotionally being with God?

When I do this meditation, I have fun going through crystal palaces in the heavens, until I come to a beaming, white light. I feel both loved and loving and a sense of being supported by something that is vast and infinite, and I become one with this.

If there are any difficulties seeing, sensing, or feeling God, or whatever your word is, ask what belief systems may be getting in the way. Ask yourself if you deserve to see or meet God—if you are *able, ready, and willing,* and whether you are attached or neutral. Are you receiving something and possibly negating your experience? Whatever your experience is, validate it and thank yourself for the experience. Keep the attitude of playfulness and spontaneity that will allow you to be open and flowing. If you need help, feel free to call me or participate in my classes.

The Upward (Earth-to-Heaven) Flow of God (Feminine)

The upward flow of Divine energy is considered the feminine aspect. It moves from earth to the heavens.

- Try standing, sitting, and lying down to test what is the easiest way for you to sense the universal energy. If standing or sitting, be sure your feet are flat on the ground and without shoes.
- Ask Mother God, your angels, and guides to assist you to feel this. Feel for a subtle sensation of energy, a subtle presence, almost like a light breeze, a tingling of energy rising through your body. Imagine the energy coming from the earth's core up through your feet, through your knees, thighs, hips, chest, neck, and upward with your

eyes focusing on the top of your head. Ask Mother God to magnify this energy so you are very aware of it.

- What happens to you when you feel this earth energy? What does it bring up for you? Explore how you feel being supported by Mother Earth. Sense her support in your body. Sense yourself being safe and wanted by Mother Earth, who is feeding you with energy. What emotions are coming up? Keep on investigating what happens in your body when you are rooted to the earth that is feeding you.
- Imagine that this energy continues to come up from Mother Earth for the rest of your life. How will this change your life?

I spontaneously found an intense earth energy coming up my body while I was meditating with John of God at the Casa in Brazil. It was like Divine Feminine Love, like the energy of Mother Mary's love. When I touched people in this state, it was like Mary putting her hand on people. One person I touched in this state had been depressed for thirty years; the next day I saw him smiling and enjoying life with a new group of friends. I was amazed by the healing energy.

Whenever I have this energy, I feel held by the earth, by Divine Love, and by Mary, and I feel relaxed. If I have a question, the energy intensifies, and I feel the right answer.

One day I went to the airport to catch a plane to leave at 7 P.M. I had contemplated staying another week with John of God in Brazil. I said to the universe, "If you want me to stay, let me know." I felt the mother earth energy in my legs stronger than ever. I felt loved and felt as though I were being told to stay. I called my travel agent in California, who said she would call right back if I could change my ticket. The rules were that one must give a 24-hour notice, not fifteen minutes notice or buy another ticket for a $1000.

Fifteen minutes before the plane was to leave, the energy in my body embraced me like never before. I felt bathed in love and sat down to relax. (Normally I would have panicked and run to the plane forty-five minutes before this.) While I was doing this, the plane took off. I was still bathed in love and feeling totally relaxed. My mind was screaming, "Are you crazy? You just missed your plane. Did you want to pay another $1000 dollars?" I couldn't believe myself, but I felt totally guided by this Divine Love.

Five minutes after the plane departed, my agent called to say the airline was willing to break the rules. I could stay another week for only a $100 penalty if I went to the airline office the next morning. I had never been so calm and assured with Divine Mother Love guiding me.

My mind started going wild in response. Who was I becoming? I wouldn't be able to recognize myself. My personality was never this trusting and relaxed. I knew myself as the person who lived on a constant adrenaline rush, racing around and constantly worrying. But was this really who I wanted to be? Wouldn't I rather be a fun-loving, peaceful person who always feels supported by Mother/Father God? How about you?

Exercise: Experiencing the Feminine Aspect of God

- See or feel yourself traveling down into Mother Earth. Visualize being inside of Mother Earth. What do you see? What sensations do you notice? How do you feel emotionally? Feel what it is like to be totally embraced inside the Mother. Do you feel nurtured, safe, and taken care of?
  I visualize the inside of earth with bright, flowing lava. The lava is like the warmest, comfiest blanket imaginable. It is wrapped around me and lights up the whole inside of the earth. I feel incredibly loved.

- After feeling totally held and fulfilled, ask Mother Earth a question.
- Allow yourself to receive the answer in whatever form—visually, hearing, sensing, or feeling.

Moved-by-Spirit

Here is a fun exercise to experience being moved by the universal energy.

- Relax your arms down by the side of your body. Ask a question. Have the left arm be one answer and the right be the other answer. Ask God, the Miraculous by whatever name you use, to move your arm with the answer Divine Will has for you. Allow yourself to be totally relaxed as you do this and let the Divine take over moving your arms. When the movement subsides, thank God for being with you.

This exercise will prime you for a later exercise in the book where you allow your whole body to be moved by Spirit. It can take time and practice to be receptive enough to allow this to happen. Here is a story to inspire you.

Letting spirit move me may have actually saved my family while on a backpack trip. We had always put a pack on our dog, so that he could carry some of our supplies, and on this particular day, the dog lost the pack which held our water filter, stove, and food for the next three days. He lost it in waist-high weeds on an immense hillside. Spirit showed me in my mind where the pack was, but I couldn't locate it visually, unable to see even a foot way. Finally realizing the impossibility of this project, I knew the only solution was to be "walked by Spirit" to the pack. I relaxed and asked Spirit to take my body and the dog to this pack. When my body came to a stop, I opened my eyes fully and found my toes were touching the pack. The dog was right there also.

It is exhilarating to do this exercise in sacred places like ancient Indian ruins in North and South America. I have been thrilled by ancient dances and rituals coming through me.

Sometimes when I put on music, I literally feel like I am being danced by the Miraculous, embraced by the Miraculous, and that I am embracing the Miraculous.

Experiencing God as Light

Fifteen years ago on a flat rock at Machu Picchu in Peru, I experienced spinning thousands of feet up out of my body to a realm of spirits made of every color of light. All had consciousnesses, were infinite light, eternal, one with God, had memories, but had no bodies. (Years later, I found out that I had meditated on a rock where they did sacrifices.) After a few hours, I came back to my body and was surrounded by hundreds of butterflies for the rest of the day. I was in an "enlightened" altered state for weeks. I had experienced my deepest truth being an eternal spirit of light and consciousness.

This was supported by an experience that happened when my husband's mother died. My son Zen (age 3) and I were sound asleep after returning from the hospital. The moment she died, her energy came through our bodies and woke us up at 1:00 A.M. She was like a bright firecracker, like a wild stallion flying high speed through us every hour (2:00, 3:00, 4:00, and 5:00 A.M.) until I said, "Stop! I get the message. You've given us the experience that we are spirits in physical bodies." She stopped waking us up after that and spun out into the universe.

Another light experience happened this year after I gave John of God (as the Entity) a photo of Christ with a poem dedicating my life to serving God and setting up a healing meditation center (which is a worldwide webinar accessed at www.holistictherapiesinc.com). When I sat down, I was blinded by light within my body. (I was surrounded by light other times while meditating.) This time, I was the light source, like a star shining, lighting up the entire universe. I sat for hours in total bliss as the full brightness of the sun. This memory saturated my cells so fully that it now happens all the time.

Exercise for Experiencing Yourself as Light

I'd like to support you to have an experience of your essence being a light spirit. In learning to do this exercise, it may be helpful to sit in the sun or moonlight or be under an indoor light. After a while, you may not need this, as the goal is experiencing yourself as the source of radiant inner light.

- Relax. Spend a few minutes sensing the energy of mother earth. Visualize light and sense energy coming up your feet to your head and feel divinely loved.
- Now spend a few minutes sensing energy and light streaming from your head down to your feet, while feeling the masculine aspect of God's love.
- Now focus on seeing a light as bright as the sun shining from within your body all around your body. Ask Mother/Father God, Christ, the angels and guides to intensify this light in and around your body and help you to perceive it grow brighter and brighter.
- Affirm this by repeating, "I am light," until you become light and you don't need to say it anymore. If your mind starts distracting you, come back to being light, sensing light, feeling light, and saying the words "I am light" over and over. See every cell in your body as filled with light.

Daily Practice

The more you practice all these exercises on a daily basis, the stronger you will see, sense, and feel Divine Love within you. Start by practicing with your eyes shut, as this is the easiest. Then practice sensing universal energy and Divine Love with your eyes partially shut, until you are able to maintain the awareness with your eyes open. Eventually concentrate being aware of this Divine Love flowing through you when you are active doing things, and then active being with other people.

At the end of the book I suggest feeling this flow of Divine Love from your heart around others and the earth as an ongoing awareness. With this awareness, you are living the Miraculous, one with Divine Love within and all around you. In this state of being filled with Divine Love and expanding Divine Love around the earth, you are living as "big Self." From this perspective, the ego fears and beliefs (discussed in the second half of the book) will be seen as the small self needing healing. Most of us are unconsciously controlled by the small self running the show. In my experience, continually feeling this flow of energy melted my negative belief systems and my ego. This made it easier to surrender to Divine Will (which we'll get to later).

Many students in my classes have said they believed in God but the *experience* of God gave them more comfort, confidence, and strength than they ever had. There was no going back. This was a transition into *living* God. One woman reported that the practice led her to feel the reality of God in a way that shook her life. Some felt loved like they never had. Clients I take to Brazil to see John of God have similar testimonials of experiencing the reality of God as one with them from then on.

Now that you have experienced yourself as light, in the next chapter you will experience yourself as a spirit that has always been infinite, eternal light.

4

What Can Be Learned from the Perspective of Dying

The Soul wants only God. Because the Soul's single motive is merging with God (p. 203).
—*Still Here, Embracing Aging, Changing, and Dying*, Ram Dass

Would you like to experience yourself as an eternal spirit, one with God?

When you live from the perspective of having experienced being an eternal spirit after "dying," you experience the oneness of the Divine along with some sense of your own individual consciousness. This is an invaluable experience, so much so that spiritual traditions often tell us to live as if we may die any minute.

The Dalai Lama tells people to practice dying every night for a month. You can repeat this—sort of like the movie *Groundhog Day* about a reporter reliving the same day over and over again until he learns the art of love. In this case, we practice the experience of dying in order to feel our true nature.

Joining My Mother's Dying

The last time I experienced the state that is beyond this life, was in Brazil. I would ask John of God (as the Entity) three questions each day. These were questions I asked for and was given by Spirit. My ordinary mind didn't have a list of questions. I knew that if I asked the wrong question, I would get the wrong answer. So each day I would say, "Thy Will is My Will, God. What is the question today?"

One day I received the question, "How do I die with my Mother?" My mother had been in a vegetative state for two years, and I wanted to help her. Still, this was a shock. I got out my Portuguese dictionary and translated the question myself so the interpreters who talk with the Entity wouldn't mess it up. The Entity was so sweet that day and listened while I spoke directly to him in Portuguese. He looked at me and motioned for me to go meditate with the other several hundred people.

For the next two hours, I found myself in a tunnel of light walking behind John of God (as the Entity) carrying my mother in his arms. We traveled up this tunnel to pure, white light and bliss.

The next day in the meditation hall, I found myself in the tunnel again. This time I was told to go to her and that she would die in three days at 2:33 A.M. After the meditation, I called Utah from Brazil. Mom had stopped eating and drinking that morning. I flew home the next morning, did the meditation with her, and she died peacefully at 2:33 A.M. Brazil time.

I realized now why the question had been to ask how to die with my mother. I "died" with her, going into a state of love and bliss. At that moment, my ego died to resisting God. All this Divine Love just melted my ego which matured into wishing only to love and be devoted to God.

I felt that God had given me one of the greatest gifts I could give to my mother—the gift of knowing God and being able to finally die in peace. I believe that she had been terrified to die, not knowing that she was a spirit and would find God. My knowing God (thanks to the Entity's help) gave her the safety she needed to leave her body and enter a spiritual paradise.

The Value of Dying and After-Life Experiences

I spent three years dying with Grave's disease. I realized that the fear that subconsciously drove my life was a fear of dying. I was not open to my highest purpose of doing healing work because any physical ailments reminded my subconscious of dying.

To my surprise, I adapted to this practice of dying. I learned how to slow down; looking at a cloud became absorbing and as big an event as climbing a mountain used to be. My sensitivity got very sharp. I was often peaceful and in bliss, except for moments I realized I was sliding away. My guidance told me that I was to heal and live. I would panic at those times and ask, "How do I heal?" In contrast, dying would have been easy, to my surprise.

To me, it is important to have these experiences for several reasons. One is that when you experience this, you find out the truth of who you are as an eternal Spirit of Divine Love. You begin to see this life as a dot on the larger continuum of your soul evolving toward divinity.

Another reason to experience dying from this realm (or birthing into the next) is to have the experience of total surrender to the process, of *letting go and letting God*. There is no turning back. For me, these practice experiences of dying made me less afraid of dying and allowed me to let go and let God guide me in being more alive. Following God's will is like a constant dying of the ego.

In fact I have gone from subconsciously being terrorized by dying and avoiding it at all costs, to consciously choosing to practice physically dying. Now why would any sane person want to practice dying by being strangled into fainting (only in a professional, supervised setting)? Perhaps your mind is now judging me as being "nuts." But to my mind, I need to know what causes me to lose awareness of being one with God, being the Divine Love that I am. Whatever limits me from being love is my growing edge. What limits you? Falling off of cliffs? Being murdered?

My experience of being strangled by someone acting hostile toward me was a highlight of my life. As I felt my blood stop, my vision blur, and my legs weaken, all I felt was unconditional love for all of humanity, for all of existence, for myself, for this person yelling at me and strangling me. My essence was infinite love and I passed out. I was challenged and elated, so I relived this same experience three more times. I felt free. There was nothing in life that I could use as an excuse to stop me from living and being the unconditional love that I am. I physically knew that our true essence is love.

Practicing confronting dying in meditation allows us to experience our essence of Divine Love. If we can die in love, we can live in love—there is nothing left to stop us.

I will tell you a story about my son, Zen, when he was age six and had a near-death experience. During school recess he was swinging upside down on the tricky bars and fell, landing on his head. He later told me how he went up a tunnel of light, met my husband's mother and many lights, and saw his entire life. Then Margaret, his grandmother, told him to go back to his body because he didn't belong there. He returned to his body and went into the school. He sat in circle as they were going around the circle, clapping. On his turn, there was no clapping to be heard. He couldn't understand what was happening, because he was patting his hands together. Then he remembered that his physical body was outside. He went out and said it was hard to get back in his body, but he did it. Then he went back into the school and sat in the circle. This time he could hear his hands clapping on his turn.

Now the problem with my son experiencing dying was that he was wiser and smarter than me, fearless and more aligned with God. So I had difficulty with him from then on. (If this is the consequence, may we all have the same consequence!) I hope this gives you courage to do the following meditation.

Dying Meditation

I would like to lead you in a process of becoming one with the light during an experience of dying. I would also like you to discover attitudes, beliefs, emotions, and body sensations during this "dying" process. This will be useful information to process in the second half of the book.

I invite you to allow this glove of the physical body to slide away on the imaginary plane as you "die" in this exercise utilizing guided imagery. In this meditation, we will take twenty minutes to approach dying and twenty minutes to be in the spiritual realm.

I did this meditation on dying before getting thyroid problems. My attention went to noticing my throat shut down and having a difficult time breathing. I kept choking, and I experienced several past lives being killed by the throat. So note what is happening as your body is shutting down, "dying," and bring this information back with you. Notice what attitudes and thoughts arise as you contemplate death. Remember these, and we'll process them in another chapter.

If you've ever had trouble returning to the here and now after exploring the spiritual realm, please find a friend to assist you in this process, buy my CD with this exercise, or join my class (see back of this book). Please agree to come back to your body when the time is up. The angels will guide you, and help keep the cord connected between your consciousness and your earth body.

- Relax your body by tightening all the muscles in your body, hold your breath, and release the muscles, as you let go of the breath. Do this again, and one last time.
- Become very tuned into your senses and awareness. Imagine going up or down sixty-five feet to get into a theta state, which is a brain wave frequency associated with a more receptive state.
- Take a minute to sense the universal energy and see sunlight going from heaven to earth inside of your body. When you are ready, practice feeling the earth energy coming up your feet through your body and on to the heavens. Continue sensing this Divine Love energy.
- Now call into your awareness whatever Divine expression speaks to you, whether Christ or Mary or any other. Watch for a new sensation. You may feel heat or tingling, or as though there is a wind blowing into your body. Ask for this to be magnified so you feel the presence more strongly. If you wish, ask Christ to open your heart. You can strengthen and affirm this by saying, "I am feeling Christ's love expanding my heart. "
- For the next twenty minutes, notice your thoughts, emotions, body sensations, and spiritual experiences. You will experience attitudes that have been with you for lifetimes. Make a mental note of these and any other important information that will help you to grow.
- Since there are many people in our lives, there may be important people for you to say good-bye to and with whom some kind of completion is needed. Perhaps you need to forgive someone or the situation is so difficult you need to hand it over to God for help.

- Have your friend give five-minute interval warnings, also prompting you to be aware of body sensations, emotions, and thoughts. Be aware of your attitudes, your emotions and your spiritual connection. (You can make notes via your helper writing down what you say.) The facilitator should count down the last minute from sixty to zero and instruct you to watch the body sensations as your body is shutting down, noticing your emotions, thoughts, and spiritual connection.
- At zero, the facilitator should tell you your cord is connected and they will be there waiting for you to return to your body in twenty minutes.
- The facilitator should give a warning at fifteen minutes for you to get ready to come back to your body.
- When the time is up, the facilitator says, "Come back into your body, and feel the heaviness of your body against the ground. Take some deep breaths."
- Take five minutes to integrate the experience and feel divinely loved.
- The facilitator should then prompt you to take more deep breaths, open your eyes, look around the room. It's helpful to walk around the room and get a drink of water.
- Write about your experience and how experiencing this has impacted your life, knowing now that you are eternal.

My Experience with the Dying Meditation

I had a life-altering experience the last time I led this meditation with a class. Spirit extended my awareness so that I was simultaneously leading, experiencing myself dying, and experiencing each person in the class dying. I was in multiple places, being all of them simultaneously. This showed me the infiniteness of being one with God's consciousness.

I'll end this chapter by sharing with you one of my experiences with this meditation. As I approached dying, I felt Spirit guiding me. I found myself feeling a profound love for my body and my life. Tears streamed down my face. I was myself as a spirit in God consciousness, seeing my life and loving it so much. I felt so grateful to my life and to my body. I loved all the places on earth I had visited. I loved everyone, all my family and friends. I loved all my pets, favorite mountains, trees, plants, homes. I was surprised by all that I loved.

This was a contrast to the previous time, when I was in fear and felt like I was not enough and sad about my life. My mind thought about all the things I wished I had done and all my fallacies. This time I felt so abundant and grateful for everything. I felt fulfilled. The difference was incredible.

I felt one with God and grateful for this oneness. What a change! I forgave myself for all the things that seemed like painful experiences. I forgave others who seemed to cause me pain. But these memories were small compared to all that I loved.

When the moment came, counting to zero, I became pure light, infinite rainbows emanating from me as a light of consciousness travelling the universe. I was pure bliss, joy, delight, and love.

I spent time seeing my life and feeling the love or pain I had given to others who were now one with me. Then to my utter shock, my feminine essence was loving myself as a masculine essence. I was Goddess loving God. Both essences were reflections of the same. I marveled in this blissful love-making.

As I was experiencing this, I was connecting to each student's spirit and leading the class. It was wild! God was showing me ten things at once. I was in awe, one with God laughing.

My only regret was realizing that we were still on earth time and it was time to bring everyone's spirit back into their bodies and to integrate all of our experiences. One of my students who read the *Tibetan Book of the Dead* related how the masculine and feminine come together during one of the phases after dying. Some students felt the sense of being one with God as eternal light; others were not prepared to let go in this way, but ended up having awesome experiences later in the week. Everyone had some sort of shift.

For the next two weeks it was as though I was enlightened in the present moment, feeling grateful for everything and in love with everything. I wrote this poem about the impact of the experience.

> *I see myself with God's eyes.*
> *I love myself.*
> *I'm so in love,*
> *So grateful for life,*
> *For my being,*
> *For all I've done,*
> *For all the places I have been,*
> *for my family,*
> *for all my friends.*
> *I am love.*
> *I am one with God.*
> *I am God loving me.*
> *I am myself loving God.*
> *I am myself loving myself,*
> *as male and female, both as God.*
> *I am Divine Love.*
> *All I have ever been is love.*
> *Love is all I am.*
> *I am One with God,*
> *One with God. One with God, one with love*
> *I am Divine Love, love, love, love*
> *Infinite Divine Love*

5

Finding Your Higher Purpose

You were made for a mission (p. 281).... Your mission gives your life meaning. William James said, "The best use of life is to spend it for something that outlasts it (p. 285).
—The Purpose Driven Life, Rick Warren

Would you like more clarity about your mission, your purpose?

Now that you have experienced being a spirit after death, you will do an exercise of being a spirit before birth and finding your higher purpose.

When I was chronically fatigued, spending eighteen hours a day in bed, one of the biggest energy boosters helping me heal was gaining a perspective of my higher purpose. As a spirit before being born into this life, I looked down on earth and saw a world full of sad people who had forgotten their Oneness with God.

I saw my life unfold. (Dr. Wayne Dyer in his book *Inspiration* recounted a similar experience.) I saw myself being put in my mother's womb. She was depressed and exhausted with four other children and didn't want another baby. I was born premature, was starving, allergic to cow's milk, colicky, crying all night, and I saw my mother get to a point of losing her patience. I saw myself at eight months old thrown against a wall when I was crying to be fed. After that, I was scared of everyone. I was so scared that I didn't talk the first five years of my life.

44

I saw in the exercise that I had become one of those sad people on earth and had lost my spiritual connection. All of this happened as part of a Divine plan. I had to go through all of this so that I could understand and have compassion for all the people I came to help. I had to heal myself and my relationship with Spirit by learning to trust and feel loved again so I could help others do the same thing.

After the exercise, I felt energized from seeing the bigger perspective of my purpose, and my healing accelerated by leaps. Now my higher purpose of becoming one with Spirit not only would heal myself, but others as well. My learning spiritually based holistic healing work would help others heal this way too. Knowing my higher purpose spurred me on into my new life.

Finding Your Higher Purpose from a Pre-birth Perspective

Oftentimes our lives don't make sense until we see our lives from the perspective of our higher purpose. There are a number of exercises that can help you identify your life purpose. This first one is the most simple and is inspired by some questions Heyoan asks in Barbara Brennan's book, *Light Emerging: The Journey of Personal Healing.* You'll want to find a comfortable place to take some time with this exercise. Do what you can to minimize distractions.

- Take your body through a relaxation using whatever techniques work for you to get into a theta state. Connect with God.
- When you've let go of everyday concerns and reached a state of relaxation, imagine that you are traveling back in time to before you were born. Travel to where you were in heaven. Go back to being spirit, infinite light in infinite time and space. Enjoy this space. Become aware of looking down on earth.

- As you look upon earth, what do you see? Is there something that you feel the earth or its people need? (You had to have seen something that you thought would benefit the earth, or you wouldn't have come here this lifetime.) Allow yourself to feel your heart, feel what is calling you to earth. What is stirring you so much that you want to help? See, sense, feel, hear, and know your purpose on earth. Take ten minutes to experience your calling here.
- Write about your experience. You can ask for more information from guidance later if you don't understand something.

What is your purpose? It may be something related to a weakness or difficulty, as it was, for example, with me. How else do you explain a person who couldn't stand to say the word *God* come to be writing this book?

My journey involved losing God, losing trust, feeling unwanted and unloved, and losing my health so I would learn how to reconnect with the Miraculous on every level. Now that I have learned to connect with God, I feel this connection is so precious and special that there is nothing that excites me more than sharing the journey with others.

Exercise: Finding a Symbol for Your Higher Purpose

A good way to find your higher purpose is to tune into your heart. Our hearts are where our soul and God meet. To raise the vibration of your heart and get the clearest answer, feel God's love opening your heart.

- To also get the clearest answer, ask for Thy Will to come through by doing a short prayer like *Thy will is my will.*
- Allow yourself to be open to whatever comes up, continuing to focus on your heart.

- Allow yourself to see a symbol that symbolizes your higher purpose on earth. Sense what is the meaning of this symbol. Feel whatever emotions it brings up. Allow it to transform into a more exact picture of what you are doing when manifesting your higher purpose.
- If you need help on this, there are angelic helpers just waiting to be asked to help. They are not allowed to interfere unless they are asked, so don't be bashful about asking.

When your heart is feeling joy and passion, this is another way Spirit is guiding you. Take a few minutes and allow the love and joy in your heart to talk to you as Mother/Father God. Have your passion visually show you what it wants, or allow yourself to verbalize your heart's passion, or allow your hand to be moved with your heart's passion or experiment with allowing your heart's passion to speak to you in all the above ways. Don't edit anything. Make a commitment to follow whatever you are shown.

What If You Had Only a Certain Amount of Time to Live? (Exercise)

If we tune into our hearts and imagine that a doctor has just told us that we have only six months to live, our true higher purpose will come through without being edited or interfered with by the mind. This is such a powerful exercise, I do it twice a year every year.

- Get a piece of paper and pencil. You'll want to also have a clock where you can see it. Give yourself twenty minutes to do this exercise.
- Time yourself for three minutes and write down everything that comes to you in response to the question, What

would you do if you had six months to live and you had no obligations to anyone or anything, no *shoulds*, and that you are free to do anything? Write at least ten items on your paper. Ready, set, go!

- Now imagine that you have one year to live. Write ten items. Then five years, fifteen, twenty-five, and a hundred years (infinite time). Take three minutes to write about each.
- Look at your list and notice what changes. Notice what stays the same. Are there certain values, themes, and purposes that you see throughout them?
- Notice if there are things that your heart prioritizes that you aren't living in your life right now. Are you inspired to change your life to live more in alignment with your heart?
- Choose to follow five to ten items on your list.

When you think of your life as limited, often your priorities get clear. I am including several exercises with different ways for you to view your life purpose.

Looking at Life Purpose from a Deathbed Perspective

Another way to get clear on our highest purpose is to look at our lives from the vantage point of our deathbed or being a spirit after death. What I love about this exercise is that in imagining (even practicing!) dying, our hearts awaken to being passionate about what is really important in life from a spiritual perspective.

- Relax and imagine that you are getting ready to die or have just died. Imagine looking back at your life. Notice your heart, and ask what you accomplished during your life. Look at how your higher purpose unfolded and how you benefited others. Look at your physical accomplishments. Look at your emotional maturing. Look at your spiritual development. Jot down some notes.

Your heart will guide you to what is most important. What are you learning doing this? Are there surprises? Are you following your heart? How do you plan to live your life now that you have done this exercise? Commit to doing some of the items on your list.

Identifying Steps to Manifest Your Purpose

Now you have a sense of your highest purpose, you will want to know the next steps to manifest it. Here are three different explorations to help you do this.

Exercise 1: God Speaking Through You

All of us are clairsentient and have access to God guiding us in all ways. You can also explore your highest purpose having Mother/Father God speak through you or to you.

- Take five minutes to relax, and go down sixty-five feet to get in a theta state.
- Visualize going into Mother Earth and being cleansed by her love and light. (If you feel called, visualize yourself purified in her fires.)
- Call in the presence of God, Christ, angels, and guides to be with you. Feel the presence of love in your body.
- Sense the universal energy going down or up through your body.
- Visualize being absorbed into the pure light of God.
- Enjoy this state and, when you feel ready and able to speak, say, "Please, God, use my voice to talk to me and use my ears to hear what is said. Thy Will is my will, God. Help me understand the next steps to manifesting my highest purposes."

- Allow an answer to come by God using your voice or hearing the soft inner voice speaking.
- Play with this until you develop a method of receiving guidance.

Most of us have developed one avenue more than others. For example, I was most receptive visually, emotionally, kinesthetic sensing, and intuiting. The hearing mode of receiving opened up immensely after I had an ear infection and couldn't hear anything externally. Is God humorous or what?

Exercise 2: Automatic Writing

You'll need a piece of paper and pencil for this exercise.

- Relax and go into a theta state. Sense God's presence.
- Say aloud, "*Thy Will is my Will.*"
- Ask God, the angels, and guides to move your hand and write down the first simple step that you are to take to manifest this higher purpose this week.
- You can half-shut your eyes if this helps you go inside. Just allow the energy within to move your hand. Take a few minutes. You've already practiced being moved with an earlier exercise, so now let yourself be moved answering this week's step to take.

Getting a Higher Perspective

It deepens our sense of higher purpose tremendously if we can also see it from a higher perspective, as Spirit might see it. I first outline the steps very simply and then provide a guided imagery exercise.

- Taking yourself into a relaxed state, ask to be shown your life from the perspective of Spirit.

- If you are currently sick or in a difficult time of your life, you can specifically ask how this is teaching you some lesson that supports your purpose.
- Ask to be shown specifically how this higher purpose is to manifest.

Here is a guided imagery exercise that may help you get a higher perspective on your purpose.

- Start by getting comfortable and putting yourself into the theta state, which you know how to do now. You feel relaxed and comfortable.
- Now imagine that you are walking in one of your favorite places. Look all around you and appreciate what you always like about this place.
- As you are walking, you notice that a feeling of anticipation grows within you. You sense that something very good is about to happen. You are near something or someone who is very wise and powerful and very loving. Let yourself sense the presence of this special wise being. It could be a mythological god or goddess, Christ, an angel, even the spirit of a tree or mountain. It may be someone you've known or your own Higher Self.
- You sense that as you walk just a little further, this being will come into full view. Let that happen now.
- Now greet this being, exchanging names. Ask what is your next step in manifesting your purpose.
- Now imagine walking up to this being, around to their backside, and entering the body of this being. Become one with this wise being. Feel their wisdom, their oneness with God, their oneness with all consciousness. Feel their unconditional love.
- Look at yourself through this being's eyes. What do you see? Speak to the seeker that is standing in front of you,

answering the question that has been put to you. If there are further questions, hear these and answer these.

- When there is a completion, leave this wise being's body and go back to being yourself facing the wise being. Thank this being for helping you.

Now that you know what your purpose is and some steps to take, here is an exercise to help you to succeed by using all of your energy and commitment.

Feeling Empowered to Succeed in Your Higher Purpose

This exercise increases your awareness of how engaging all four levels of your being empowers you. You push against a wall with a quick movement and notice how far you rebound from the wall. (My friend Cosme Castanieda, who wrote *The Kiss of God*, teaches this.)

- Now *think* of fulfilling your higher purpose as you push off a wall. Notice how much energy you feel. How far did you go from the wall?
- Now *emotionally feel* your love for your higher purpose and repeat pushing off the wall and notice how far you went.
- Now *physically feel* your determination for your higher purpose and repeat pushing off the wall and notice how far you went.
- Now feel *spiritually guided* to fulfill your higher purpose as God's higher purpose and repeat pushing off the wall and notice how far you went.
- Finally, feel spiritually guided, physically determined, emotionally full of love, and mentally "jazzed" to fulfill your higher purpose, and repeat pushing off the wall. Notice how far you went. Engaging all four levels of energy should have given you the furthest push away from the wall.

In my classes, people find their energy triples using all levels of involvement. By physically experiencing full commitment on all four levels, you will automatically remember this and do it. You'll want to work at balancing all four levels, especially the lowest level.

Saying Yes to Higher Purpose

You agreed to fulfill your and God's higher purpose in God's way and in God's timing. It will unfold as God's Will with God's support. Normally we get our egos involved and want to push and complete goals as they make sense to our egos. Let the Great Mystery be your new guide. Meditate and receive guidance, look for guidance, flow with guidance. Be open to a new way of having your life unfold. We will continue to work with being able to live spiritually connected to God rather than "edging God out" as Wayne Dyer calls it.

Sometimes we get guidance that we don't understand and are tempted to "edge God out." When this fear sets in, ask God to confirm the guidance you are getting. Two years ago I asked Spirit to give me a vision of my next purpose to fulfill. But when I received a vision of being on stage with Christ using me to do individual healings as well as connecting the entire 2,000 people in the audience to God and healing them too, I almost fainted with terror. I said, God, if you exist, you'd better help me say your name without vomiting and help me fulfill this vision. This is way harder than dying and coming back to life.

God heard this because three days later I was being danced on stage in front of 2,000 people. Three more days and I had three clients in my office giving me two videos and photos of John of God in Brazil. I figured a man with a name like this definitely must know God and would help me find God, too. I never in my wildest dreams imagined myself of all people writing a book about connecting with God. I now know God has a sense of humor!

I was a happy, peaceful closet healer before I asked for this guidance. I tried to pretend the vision was just my ego's idea so I could dismiss it, but God confirmed the guidance in such huge ways I had to follow and went to Brazil instead. All I did was say "yes," and you will see what has happened in two years. I had not planned to teach, only to do individual healings.

But confirmations about my teaching also happened. The day I asked about teaching, I was (synchronistically) given a job teaching a class on synchronicity. Two hours later, I participated in a demonstration of a psychic reading technique and was told that my highest calling was being a teacher bringing spirit from heaven to earth through my heart and through love.

The next week a friend told me to buy Harv Ecker's book, *The Secret of the Millionaire Mind*. When I picked up his book, I had a vision of teaching with him. I didn't know who he was, if he was aligned with God, or if he had a teaching program. Immediately I read his book and found he followed "Higher Self" and was dedicated to supporting people to live their potential, becoming financially free and serving the world.

This fit a previous vision I had about opening up to receiving money in order to be used by God however God wanted me to serve people in their healing. I opened to doing healing presentations for Harv, in churches, on web videos, on a web audio collection—anywhere I was guided. Next I was guided to take three years of Harv's classes for $29,000. I wished I could edge God out on this one, because I had a lot of work to do believing and feeling abundant. I had just committed to saving money to create a way to do donation healing; now I was guided to spend what I feared was way, way too much.

But, luckily for me, Harv's Millionaire Mind Intensive helped me connect with my financial blueprint of money being linked to subconscious sadness. Money meant not having loving relationships with people nor with Spirit. Money meant worrying and not having fun in life from watching my parents and their friends. I had fifty amazing negative beliefs about money that would have never allowed me to create a worldwide web video, audio collection and webinars.

I also read Audrey Craft Davis' books, *Making Love with God: The Art of Mental Connection* and *Prosperity Consciousness: A Metaphysical Guide to Your Natural Wealth*. These are fabulous books and helped me really become even more of a partner with God, expecting more miracles than ever before, sharing God's Kingdom, a Cosmic Bank Account and signing contracts with God.

Then I took Harv's Life Directions class and shared my mission to help everyone to connect with God by all names and attain optimal health physically, mentally, emotionally and spiritually. You have to remember that only two years before, I couldn't say the word God, and to tell a stranger that my mission was connecting people with God royally embarrassed me. God was playing a joke on me and for three days I had to tell a hundred people, directly looking into their faces, my mission.

The next workshop I stretched to meeting Harv Ecker and told him I was impressed that in five minutes, a thousand people felt open and safe to give each other loving hugs and share from the bottom of their hearts. I told him Peak Potentials was my family and that I wanted to teach my mission of how to connect with universal love, God by all names, and help people attain optimal health at his next Extreme Health class. I was able to say this without being embarrassed due to my three days of practicing.

When you say yes to God, rather than edging God out, God moves you right along, as you can see from my story here. Next I was guided to do classes with Dr. Kam Yuen to complete my certification in Yuen Method Chinese Energetics. Dr. Yuen asked me my goals. One was rasing two million dollars for a meditation healing center to have one to two thousand people receive healings at a time. I described how this felt out of reach for another three to five years. Kam is a miracle-worker though. He did a correction and asked me to feel the difference. Now I felt all of this could be a reality at this moment. My out-of-reach goal was in reach. Several months later when I was Kam's guide to meet John of God at the Casa, the healing center grew into a webinar center serving the world!

He asked for my next goal. I said I wanted to live Christ love and consciousness. His next correction for myself and the roomful of students getting certified to teach Yuen Method was not having a problem being enlightened. We spent four days releasing everything that kept us from unconditional love. Can you imagine feeling the freedom of having no problems? Go one more step. Imagine the freedom of having no problem with having no problems. I had asked the Entity to help me live Christ love and consciousness and was told God would help me, and God put me on the fast-track for sure. The next month I learned Harv's template for teaching to a thousand people in an audience.

Every day I say yes, God, use me for the highest purpose, love and joy. Do you want to have your life make a difference on earth? Yes? Then just say the magic words: "Yes, God, I am fulfilling my highest purpose aligned with you."

Using Numerology as an Aid

Another way to confirm your higher purpose and steps that you receive in meditation is by having an astrology or numerology session. You can learn numerology somewhat simply by buying a book such as *Numerology and the Divine*

Triangle by Faith Javane (very detailed) or *Helping Yourself with Numerology* by Helyn Hitchcock (simpler).

The vowels in your name will indicate your soul or heart longings; the consonants indicate your personality. Your destiny (what you must do this lifetime) is ascertained by looking at the vowels and consonants together.

To know the summation of how your life looks, you add you birth date to your destiny and get your power number. You can check out how the meditations we have done match what your name and birth date indicates.

When you have developed some sense of your higher purpose, you can better understand that Spirit might need to use some detours to develop additional talents that you might need. It is often amazing how things that seem inconsequential in our lives, or even like distractions, end up being something that was a perfect and necessary step in our larger journey. Now that you are more in touch with your higher purpose, we'll spend the next chapter motivating you to see how guidance I received and followed, regardless of how "bizarre and crazy" my mind judged it to be, led to miraculous happenings. Then you will be ready for the next chapter, following guidance regardless of your mind's judgments about detours and it not making sense.

6

Living in Alignment with Divine Love and Will

I can only call this feeling (with Jesus) adoration. It was more complete than any love I had known, and it was love so pure as to have a sound and a fragrance.
—Love Without End ... Jesus Speaks, Glenda Green

How would you like to live more aligned with Divine Love and Will?

In my case, it was tangible experience of the Divine, which led to a more solid love connection with the Miraculous, and this led to a deep devotion. In this chapter, I'll share with you several stories about how this has worked in my life, and in the next chapter, I'll give you tools to help you follow your own guidance.

I wish I could say that I am totally relaxed with guidance and have no fear. My hope is that practice makes it easier. Even with all my love and devotion, following some of my guidance takes "guts" and all my courage. I share this so you will understand that it is a journey, a process of total devotion, courage, love, and constantly learning to trust ourselves and Spirit.

No Use Resisting

There is a difference between living life inspired by fear and by ego versus inspired by love. It is the difference between living life according to my will or according to Thy Will (of God or Higher Self, which is one with God).

Here is an example of my ego fighting with God in 1986 and not being aligned. I had a vision of a home I saw myself buying, yet I was without money, living in a sleeping bag in the hallway of a house filled with other people. I had given away, lost, and been robbed of all my money. I was pissed off and told Spirit not to give me visions of what I can't have. Don't tease me, I said. I fucked up, and this isn't funny. I was mad at this vision and refused to follow it, having decided it was impossible

Soon I was kicked out of this house and then another house. Obviously Spirit was going to kick me out of living anywhere but this vision. I decided to give Spirit a chance and realigned with Spirit.

I went to a realtor and pointed on a map to where I knew my vision home was. "Is there a road here?" I asked. He said there was, and we hopped in the car and drove up a windy mountain road for a half hour. Why did God want me up here in the middle of nowhere?, I wondered. We went by several houses.

"How will you know the house?" the realtor asked.

I said it has dance in it and big rocks on a hill.

As we passed the next house, he said, "You don't want that one."

"That's the one!" I replied, recognizing it instantly. I could feel the dancing in the living room and the drum beat. Out back was a maypole and big rocks. This was the house—a dream come true, if I had the money.

I got the idea to ask Spirit how much to offer, just as I always asked Spirit how much to charge for my artwork.

$127,000 came to mind. The realtor said no way would he put that offer in when they were asking $157,000. It didn't matter; I didn't have the money anyway.

I told the man if he wouldn't make the offer, I'd get another realtor, because that was the price Spirit gave me. He thought I was nuts to begin with and was getting more convinced by the minute. I thought I was nuts too, but not following Spirit had gotten me kicked out of two houses. I had no choice but to keep on asking Spirit what to do.

A few days later the offer was accepted with a nonrefundable $10,000 earnest money due in ten days. In the meantime I had six months to get a loan.

I arranged to pay rent and moved into the house. Immediately I advertised for housemates who were into creativity, healing, and spirituality, since in my vision, this was the theme of the house. The housemates showed up and helped pay the rent. The earnest money of $10,000 showed up out of the blue from my father who said he had just sold a business that I was part of and here was my share.

Now I needed the loan. I tried for six months to get a loan, but no one wanted to give a loan to an artist without a structured job. I prayed and did prayer circles, asking that if it was the highest purpose, I would get the house.

Two weeks before losing the house and earnest money, a loan agent apologized, saying, "I can't help you, but do you mind if I send it to a friend?"

"Do anything." I said.

The day before losing my house, I got a phone call from the "friend" who said that his boss was giving me the loan. The boss's secretary was my father's neighbor in Utah. She told him that I must be a good person like my father and told him to sign the loan. He did.

It was an act of God to be sure. It was an act of testing my trust in the vision that I had been shown by Spirit.

God Finds a Way

God is persistent, luckily for me. We all know that some-times it takes persistence to accomplish something. Well, it took a lot of persistence to hitch me up with my soul mate because he didn't fit my pictures of the man I would marry.

I had prayed to find my soul mate and been told that my soul mate lived very near. One day as I ran through the little mining town of Gold Hill where I live, a large dog bit me. I was mad. I got the owner's name (Chuck) and called him to tell him to keep his dog at home. He wasn't very compliant. Instead, he told me not to run through Gold Hill again. I was fit to slug this man; I had never had anyone be so arrogant to me in my life.

The dog next appeared at my bedroom window. I saw him getting my dog pregnant, my purebred that was only six months old and that I did not want pregnant yet—especially with *that* dog. My housemate Crystos had let my dog out accidentally. I called up Chuck and demanded that he take his dog home. He said it was impossible, because the dog ate through metal chains, but he would do his best.

I went out of town and when I returned, the dog was in my house as Crystos's adopted pet. I called up Chuck. He said Crystos had begged him to let him have this dog. If I got rid of the dog, Crystos would leave brokenhearted. I could not believe it. The dog stayed, living in my home.

That winter my boyfriend and I were on our way skiing when we came upon a hitchhiker with skis. Guess who? Chuck climbed into the car, and I proceeded to yell at him the next two hours all the way to Loveland ski resort and back. I hated this man. But he was blind, only seeing fuzzy silhouettes in black and white, and I had a laying-on of hands healing group at my house, so I invited him to get free weekly healings. My hate did not destroy my compassion. For five years we were friends; I helped him however I could.

When he finally got a cataract operation and could see clearly, I invited him to go cross-country skiing with my household community. The two of us came upon a meadow with over a hundred ravens. I asked Spirit what the meaning was, as this many ravens always meant a major transformation in my life. I received the message that he was my soul mate. I laughed and asked Carlos (my name for him) what he received. He wouldn't tell me. I told him I got that he was my soul mate and then told him a hundred reasons why he wasn't and that God must have wanted to have a laugh. He told me why he would never marry me either (although he had actually gotten the same message).

It changed something though, and that night we experienced a startling intimacy with each other and seemed to find new eyes through which we saw the other. We ended up getting married and had our son, Zen. I am glad God found a way to reach me. It seems the universe will use anything at its disposal—even mad dogs.

Baptized by Spirit

My life has been about my ego fighting for control over my big Self (God-self). At some point I noticed that my Self, which focused on love, had better ideas than my ego-self, which focused on fear. After drawing a picture of my life, I noticed that everything that stood out was related to miraculous spiritual experiences. I have had many close calls with death, but my visions, gut feelings, inner voice, heart desire, and connection with Spirit saved my life. Although it was scary to follow Spirit, it was costly and painful when I didn't. One day I concluded that Spirit was wiser than my ego and following Spirit was a good idea.

I will give an example of how different I felt living my life this way. I was at John of God's Casa in Brazil. I asked him to help me sense, see, hear, and feel God, to be moved in every way by God, and to know God exactly in every way without a doubt. The Entity was wonderful that day. When I asked this question, he asked, "Exalto?" (Exactly?) I said, "Sim, exalto" (yes, exactly).

I was on a higher purpose to find God after a lifetime of not even being able to say the word *God*. My relationship with Christ was good, and I followed Spirit, but I wanted to know God and have it be tangible. I wanted to do healing work and be open to every name used for God, so any name that my clients used would work as well. I had given myself three months to become in love with God and know this God by all names.

That day, I came up from the waterfall at the Casa, blessing myself with this prayer of aligning with God and letting go of my will and all other blocks, including my resistance to the word *God*.

During meditation at the Casa with the Entity, I had an image of a long pole placed in a deep hole with gold underneath it that I felt inspired to find. In front of me a man was selling a map of the surrounding area. I felt guided to buy this map. I looked on the map and watched my hand go to a certain area.

Next to me was a parked taxi with a driver, who only spoke Portuguese. I went into a bookstore and bought a Portuguese dictionary. I then told the taxi driver in broken Portuguese that I was looking for something, and it would take 6 to 8 hours. I quoted the price that God had authorized me to pay. He motioned for me to get in the taxi, and we were off to pick up his wife for an adventure into the unknown.

I had made a commitment to following the guidance one hundred percent now in spite of my fears. In the past, my fears would have dominated my mind. I would have worried that I would not succeed at this pole in a hole, I would get lost, I would not be able to talk Portuguese, I would waste a large amount of money on nothing, I would feel humiliated and embarrassed when my friends asked what I had done, this taxi driver and his wife would laugh at me ... (and on and on). The mind will continue racing a million miles an hour if we allow it. Yet in my new life dedicated to being 100% aligned with God, I simply followed, looked at the scenery, enjoyed the present, meditated on the space, the light, the joy within me that felt so aligned with God.

Hours went by. I felt guided and the taxi driver felt aligned with my higher purpose. (He was one of the Casa drivers.) We went on all sorts of roads. The place where my hand had been guided was supposedly flooded with water. So I said let's get as close a possible, and we went toward this Saint Maria site.

One place we stopped, I saw a six-inch miniature of the pole in a hole, and I knew we were on track. Within fifteen minutes, my heart was pounding; I felt we were getting close to whatever it was that I was being guided toward. I got out and walked around; my body felt eager to continue in a particular direction.

When we came up over a barren red-clay hill, I felt pulled down the rainforest valley. The taxi driver pointed in the direction I was so intensely focused on. We found a road that went there, which took us another half-hour. There we found a pole in the hole with a brick-making device in a clay mine. I was elated. I had been guided through the unknown, exalto (precisely), and I felt connected with God totally within and all around me. But where was the gold?

Near the old brick-making area was a contemporary church. The taxi driver went to get the keys for it from the caretakers who lived next door. When the caretaker opened the church doors, I almost died laughing. There was a baptismal pool as big as a swimming pool. Here was the water that everyone along the road kept telling us about. I understood immediately that the "gold" represented my being baptized and connected with Christ, God, the Holy Spirit.

In retrospect, there were many signs pointing to this baptism experience. On the bus to the airport earlier on that trip, the lady next to me told me how she had been saved by Christ because her father had baptized her. The day before I had arrived at the Casa, the Entity had been baptizing people. To top off this baptism theme, I had had three flat tires while traveling in southern Utah on a Sunday. The only man in town with tires had to go to his son's baptism for an hour before he could help us.

I pulled out the spare shirt I was carrying which had Christ's picture on it, and I walked into the water. "Thy Will is my will. Guide me to be baptized and connected to you for life."

And so I had my private baptism with God and Christ that day in the middle of nowhere, exactly where I was guided to be, without a doubt. This funny experience is a great metaphor for living life aligned with God, with the Miraculous.

When we live in this surrendered way, we feel blessed regardless of what life brings us. We feel relaxed, trusting that all that is happening is perfect and is teaching us unconditional love. When we notice ourselves judging and closing our hearts, we forgive others, ourselves, or the situation, and ask to understand how we are growing more unconditionally loving. When we don't know where or why we are doing something, we continue to follow, trusting this Higher Intelligence within and all around us.

The Ascent of Faith

I came from a family where having a vision would have been seen as being psychotic. I think you'll understand, then, why this story is so impressive to me. For me to receive a vision, have some stranger explain it, and then do something half-way around the world I had never been before (climbing with ice axes and ropes) is pretty miraculous.

By the time this happened, I had been having visions for some time. I had worked with Beautiful Painted Arrow Joseph Rael, an Indian shaman, for years and opened up to accepting the visions I saw. One day in 1986 I had a vision of hiking up high glacier mountains that were very green at the base. I didn't understand where these mountains were, as I had never seen them before.

The next day, I heard a knock at my door and opened it to find a stranger who called himself John Able. He said that he had been guided to come to me and explain a vision I had had the day before. My eyes opened wide. I was shocked, but I listened.

I had been having experiences with three-sided, rock tetrahedrons. He said these tetrahedrons were for rituals I was to do on mountain tops. I remember little else of what he told me that day except that the mountains I saw were the Andes in Peru. I forgot everything else until after I climbed Illimani Peak in Peru in 2006 and finally understood the ritual I had been doing for twenty years of putting energy into the rock tetrahedrons. I bless the rock with prayers for world love, love for ourselves and each other, gratitude, being connected to God, abundance, success, forgiveness, and being present.

When I was on top of Illimani, I saw the prayers being blown by the wind all around the world and being breathed in by everyone. I saw the prayers go down through the rain and glaciers into the streams and plants and the water that people all over the world drink. It wasn't until this last peak, that I saw how one person doing a small gesture can have a large vibrational impact on the planet and so many people.

I felt that Illimani, the peak of illumination, was a completion of the over one hundred and fifty 14,000 to 22,000-foot peaks I've climbed doing these prayers.

How I climbed Illimani is an equally amazing story. When I had climbed peaks in the past, I had prepared by hiking, getting in shape, and acclimatizing. This particular spring, my son had been depressed about school and not into getting out in nature on weekends, so I had been inside the house. Then I got a bad ear infection and was in bed. My guidance was to go see John of God. I tried to book a ticket to Brazil, but couldn't get a price quote until I followed the next piece of guidance to go climb in Bolivia. The second I got the Bolivia ticket and climb set up, the Brazil ticket manifested.

I was afraid because I was in terrible shape, and I hadn't climbed to 21,000 feet since before dearly dying with Grave's disease. Doctors had said I'd be dead and my heart would never work again. Climbing to 21,000 feet is an exceptional strain on the heart! In going to see John of God, I was going down to an altitude of around 3,000 feet (rather than the 8,300 feet I live at) and this would be the opposite of what I should have been doing. Also, what if John of God as the Entity gave me an invisible surgical operation that would further put me out of commission right before the climb?

Sure enough, even though I tried to cancel my worst fear, the Entity sent me to get one of these astonishing operations two days before leaving for Bolivia. (One of these experiences is shared in Chapter 13 in "The Divine at Work.")

After the surgery, I was laid up in bed with no energy whatsoever. I asked what the meaning of this was. I got that "I" was not the one who would be climbing the mountain. God was the doer climbing through me; now I would be very clear about this because my body was not in shape to climb. When I got to Bolivia, I had to take it easy for another six days, once more following the Entity's stern orders, since I got food poisoning and was too weak to climb.

Right before the climb, I was given a special lesson. The night before leaving Brazil, my Nikon camera broke, displaying the word *Error*. I called many Nikon dealers and users in the states. No one knew how to fix it. A girlfriend offered me her camera since I had been guided to take photos of the top of the peak for this book. I read on the airplane that this Error message meant that only a Nikon factory could fix it. I surrendered. "Okay God, Thy Will is my will. What do you want me to do with my camera? Do I leave it at the hotel or what?"

A voice in my ear said, "Ask me to fix it."

So I asked God to fix it. I saw Christ's hands come in and work on the interior of the camera and lens almost as fast as lightening. The voice said, "It is fixed. Turn on the camera." I turned on the camera, half expecting the flashing error sign that had been a constant for the last twenty-four hours. The camera was fixed and worked perfectly. I asked if it would stay working and was told it was totally fixed and to leave my girlfriend's camera behind because it was not necessary now.

This was the third time this trip I was told to say, "Thy Will is my will" and then ask for God's help. The other two times, similar instantaneous miracles had taken place. I was being primed to repeat, "Thy will is my will" and then to ask for help climbing.

I did make it up to the top of Illimani. God saw to that, despite my weakened physical condition, despite my not being acclimatized, despite my not having climbed on ice that was this technical, and against what I considered all odds with my heart and body. At the top, I did the ritual described above.

My final lesson was the day after returning from Illimani. I went to the airport two hours early to find out that a few days before they had changed the schedule and the airplane had already left the dock and was taxing down the runway. The other flights had also left. My only choice was to buy new tickets and leave two days later on the next flight out of La Paz. I asked God, "Am I to stay here?" I could not find any urgings in my body to stay. As I was taught, I then asked what God wanted me to do. God's response was that I was complete in Bolivia and I was to leave.

I turned to the ticket agent, "You've got to help me." The next words blurted out of my mouth in spite of me. "Call the pilot and tell him to come back and get me."

Five minutes later the agent tells me that the pilot turned the plane around and was on his way back to get me. I ran up the airplane stairs greeted by a stewardess who said, "God must be with you."

"God is definitely with me," I told her.

I asked the Entities, whom I consider as messengers of Christ, why they didn't give me the heads-up to get to the airport earlier to prevent this mix up. They told me that I wouldn't have received the same lesson. The lesson was to know that God is more real than my physical body and can move airplanes and mountains. I was to know beyond a doubt how much God loved me and how much God was devoted to helping me. Greater than all of my devotion to loving and serving God, God was devoted to helping me. I wept. Truly, I felt loved and blessed by God every minute of the trip and especially with the bonus miracle of making it to the top of Illimani. It was indeed an ascent of faith.

Unending Miracles

There are so many stories I could share from my visiting John of God eight times in eighteen months. In the beginning, my mind might interpret a situation as being to my detriment, only for me to find out how God was always serving my highest spiritual evolution.

An example was when I had had surgery and wasn't supposed to carry any heavy weight. I had a heavy bag and a heavy crystal to carry. God took care of the heavy bag because immediately the airline lost it, so I never carried it again. It showed up at my doorstep hours after I got home from Brazil. The crystal was also taken care of in a very unusual creative solution. Security considered it a bomb and spent twenty minutes unwrapping it until I was late for the plane on the opposite side of the airport. Since I was going to miss my plane, security drove me in the special airplane cart with my crystal to my destination. I never had to carry the crystal.

These are just some of the miracles that have happened. Since committing myself to *Thy Will*, my life seems like unending miracles. This is not to say it is all easy; in fact, I would say there have been more challenges. But these challenges have led to finding meaning and tremendous growth. I am constantly challenged to grow more loving and more conscious, to evolve spiritually. I think this is why we are all here. It all begins with learning to trust and follow guidance, and this is what we turn to next.

7

Learning to Trust and Follow Guidance

Learn to be quick to follow that flow of love God puts in your heart. Be sensitive and obedient to do what God wants you to do. You won't be sorry—not now, or a million years from now (p. 249).

God knows what He's doing. He can see the big picture. He can see the future. And He has you exactly where He wants you today. Quit questioning Him and start trusting Him. Just know that God is in control. He has your best interests at heart. He's directing your steps (p. 281).

—*Your Best Life Now: 7 Steps to Living at Your Full Potential*, Joel Osteen

Would you like to trust God within you more?

You can see from the many stories I've shared how following guidance has changed my life. In this chapter, I'll give you some concrete suggestions and important principles related to following your own guidance.

Avenues for Receiving Guidance

There are so many different ways to have God communicate with you. I encourage you to experiment with several and find your favorites. Play, have fun, don't take yourself seriously, be as a child being shown a new game.

You can also tell God what kinds of guidance you want. If you wish to see events ahead of time, ask for this. What would you like information about?

The most basic rules are these: Become quiet, go down into the theta state, feel God's love fill your heart. Sense God's presence running heaven to earth through your body (Chapter 3); see yourself filled with light, and affirm, "Thy Will is My Will." Be open and allow yourself to receive information about your question.

The most common avenues for God to communicate with us are to use our sight and capacity for imaging (giving us a vision), use our voices (talking through us), use our ears and inner hearing (speaking to us in words), and our bodies (moving us).

You can ask God to guide you by speaking through your mouth. Ask a question. Allow words to come through your voice without judging or editing them. Or, if you want God to write through you, start by writing a question to God. Then tune into God. Affirm, "Thy Will is My Will." Allow your hand to be moved and write a response back.

Spirit may also use our hearts (for example, feeling joy), use our intuition (gut feelings), and speak through our body urges.

Moved by Spirit

To help you to approach guidance in a playful, spontaneous way with no expectations, think of where you'd like to be moved by Spirit, doing a dance celebrating your willingness to play. What music would fit this occasion?

I will share a story about myself being danced by Spirit, volunteering as a fool in front of 2,000 people with Bobby Mc-Farren. I was told by one of my clients to see Bobby McFarren, an African man who makes vocal sounds and uses his chest as a drum. That day I saw the ad for that evening's performance, so I got #35 on the waiting list. An hour later I was buying what I judged to be ridiculously expensive tickets. My son Zen and I went and were amazed when we sat down nine rows from the stage. I didn't know who Bobby was or what to expect. Bobby McFarren came out. His African chanting put me in a trance. He asked for someone to come up and dance. I felt carried by angels up to the stage. I must have looked funny there in my heavy snow boots and cranberry Peruvian coat. My son slid underneath the seat. He was ten years old. "No, Mom. Don't! I am so embarrassed!"

At the top of the stairs I realized that I was on stage and my mind was beginning the thought, "I'm not a professional dancer. What am I doing up here?"

Before I could run away, Bobby asked if I was going to dance in my snow boots. I took off my boots and he started chanting. My body was moved by his chanting as well as by the angels. I was in love with the tones and flew around the stage for twenty minutes. I was being wildly, passionately moved. Only movement and music existed until the sounds stopped, and I was in an eagle-like posture, bowing.

When Bobby hugged me, I realized that he was in a deep meditation and was one with God. About a hundred people thanked me after the concert, and I later understood that they were thanking me for being carried by God and that magnified their connection with God.

Now that you've heard my story, find your own courage.

• Put on some music and ask to be moved through the form of dance. You might decide to go out in nature or find some sacred spaces, and let the Spirits move you.

I ask that only beings of light move me. If I don't feel love, joy, fun, and aspects of God, I tell the beings to leave and light beings to come in. I have only been moved by darkness once after being around someone who dwelled on evil beings and I allowed some subconscious fear to come into me. I told the beings to leave me and that I was never available for this energy ever again in my life. Since that time, I have never felt this fear again. Trust in God, know that God is love within you, and you will always be moved by God. If, instead, you choose fear, then fearful energies will move you. It's your choice, since all of us have free will.

Building Confidence by Remembering Positive Examples

You can develop more trust in God by acknowledging when you have succeeded in the past when following guidance. Here are some examples from my own life that have been instructive to me.

In high school, I was helped to develop a mountaineering club. A group of us were excited to do an overnight snowshoe to a Girl Scout cabin in Parleys Canyon, Utah, just over the Big Cottonwood divide. It was Washington's Birthday, and the weather forecast was for sunny skies all three days. Some of the group was new to hiking and camping, so we were starting with a super-easy trip only about three miles long. We took light loads, with only our sleeping bags and a little food, because the cabin we were going to had everything else.

Off we started for a thrilling weekend together. It was totally unexpected when we crossed the divide and clouds came in and it started to blizzard. The two parent chaperones and their daughter reassured us that they had hiked this two hundred times in the summer and could walk it blindfolded. So we continued. Soon there was a foot of snow and it was not stable on the slick snow underneath. Then there was two feet of snow. To make a long story short, we were stuck camping in our sleeping bags under trees with nothing to eat.

That night the sleeping bags got wet and became solid ice bags. In the morning, the snow was four feet deep and it was still coming down hard. We decided to head back.

For one second, I looked up and saw a crack in the snow above us. I looked hard and wished for a second view before the blizzard closed back in. I just knew we couldn't go back, and I had a bad gut feeling about it.

We had two miles to get to the car by a route where I saw the avalanche waiting to happen and thirteen miles if we went down a different way. We were traveling only a half-mile an hour, with six feet of new snow. Due to my persistence in following my knowing, we chose the long way.

We did survive another night and a record of twelve feet of snow in two days. My parents got a helicopter in to rescue us during one of those short fifteen-minute breaks in the blizzard. Because of us, thirty other people were dropped food and rescued the next day after three more feet of snow fell. The avalanche did happen at some point, and the next summer the road had to be rebuilt where I saw the crack in the snow. Can you think of a time when your gut feeling or guidance saved your life or many lives?

Years later on another camping trip, wading ankle deep down the Little Colorado in hot, dry weather, I experienced a vision that again saved my life. It started to get cloudy. My ex-husband and I had gone about eight miles down this beautiful narrow Grand Canyon stream and were sitting on a rock eating granola bars. I started to filter water but kept getting an image of the river going over my head. I couldn't get the scene out of my mind. I felt a terrible gut feeling like I have never had before. I told him, "We've got to get to a cave on the cliff immediately or we'll die. It's going to flood, run."

We ran with our packs as fast as we could. He asked where the cave was. I didn't know, but I saw it and felt it inside my body and was taken involuntarily to it. About three-fourths of a mile up, I started climbing the cliff on the opposite side of the Navajo trading post, not knowing where exactly I was going. I went around a rock and screamed, "Cave! Here's our camp spot."

About three in the morning, I awoke to a roar. The river was about one hundred times wider than it had been and five to eight feet deep. It took three days clinging to cliffs and going through quicksand to get out, but we were alive.

Before going on the trip, I kept getting the feeling of a hard trip that wasn't going to be fun, but my mind overrode this guidance, and I went anyway. Thank God I listened the next time! Recalling events like these in our lives helps us to develop trust.

Can you remember other times in your life a vision, gut feeling, voice, movement, a sign, a knowing that guided you and made an enormous difference in your life? In someone else's life?

Following Guidance

We can learn to follow guidance by making the decision to do so, but trust is usually something that develops over time. We start by practicing following guidance. This was how it was for me.

I did an experiment and asked for guidance about every decision, saying, *Thy will is my will,* and following whatever guidance I received. It didn't matter if I thought it was a good idea or not, or if it looked socially acceptable. I did things I never imagined doing in my life. But a promise to God is a promise, and I had made a promise to follow one hundred percent. The only way I succeeded in following was to let go of my judgments and trying to predict outcomes.

This may be an experiment you are willing to take up, too. I made my experiment more difficult at the same time by asking the Entity to release all my fears. If I had it to do over again, I would have stayed with one step at a time. Both of these experiments in combination led to overly dramatic and many times comical experiences. I have a lot of stories and private laughs about doing some of the crazy things I did. I had been a grave person with Grave's disease. God got me laughing again, howling out of control, at feeling so scared and doing things that seemed ridiculous to my ego. I see now that I was being trained to encounter all my fears regardless of what I looked like. I found out that my terror and fear did not kill me. Even though I embarrassed myself a great deal, I found out that people loved, accepted, supported, and forgave me, and I felt free in a way I had never been in my entire life.

It helped to remind myself that nothing I did could be "wrong" because I took everything as a spiritual lesson. I did not know or concern myself with the long-term physical consequences of what I was doing, but simply followed, much like our picture of the sage having no opinions of right or wrong. In retrospect, miracles happened in all areas of my life. It also helped to remind myself that from a spiritual perspective all that I am is Divine Love and light, and the fear is ultimately not real. Nothing could hurt me.

Perhaps following guidance is difficult for you, and what may be helpful is to learn to just push through the fear. This experiment served me in many ways to follow 100 % in spite of fear.

Exercise: Following Guidance in Spite of Fear

- Get into a meditative state.
- Ask God to guide you in some small step you can take to practice learning to trust guidance.
- Commit to taking this step despite your fear.
- Do it!

- Celebrate your success in following guidance. Congratulate yourself. Jump up and down. Give yourself pats and hugs. Tell yourself what a good job you did. (You do this so your memory of following guidance is connected with celebration.)
- Repeat this exercise with larger, more important areas of your life.

If you have a spiritual teacher whom you love and who is a model for you of surrendering to the Divine, you might insert another step into this process. Make it step 2. After entering a meditative state, feel your love for your teacher and your teacher's love for you. Place your teacher in your heart and feel their courage within you. Then ask God to guide you.

You might also consider reading Gloria Green's book, *Love Never Ending*. Green had a vision of painting a picture of Christ. She was used to working only with live models and didn't know how it would be possible to do this. But she ended up painting a picture of Christ as he sat in front of her for a month and talked to her. This seemed like such an improbable thing to her, but this painting is now famous and hangs in the Smithsonian. The Miraculous is beyond the imagination of what our minds think is possible.

A psychic, singer Danae Shanti, once channeled to me that our job is just to be connected to God and follow guidance, even if guidance says to walk backwards in circles for ten years. The results aren't our business; they are only God's business. She said it is important that we commit to God one hundred percent, following all guidance. She went on to say that we can ask God to stop us and make it obvious when we are not to follow what we perceive as the guidance, if for some reason we misunderstand it. In a way, this is like an insurance policy and may make the learning quicker. That way we are assured of God helping us if we mess up.

An ultimate experience in learning to push through all your obstacles of fear on all levels is the Enlightened Warrior Camp created by Harv Ecker and put on by Peak Potentials. It is a truly amazing experience for learning how to have an open heart while embracing fear and fighting for your life's mission. Whatever fears we use not to follow our Higher Selves in our daily living is brought up in this camp. We have so many fears in our minds which are used to protect us and keep us comfortable from change. One of my favorite books, *Shambala: Sacred Path of the Warrior* by Chogyam Trungpa, a Tibetan lama and founder of Naropa University, explains how the enlightened warrior is the tender-hearted warrior who feels everything rather than the shielded warrior defending himself.

When Fear Is Paralyzing

Sometimes we want to follow guidance but are simply too afraid. The fear is paralyzing. It is also possible that pushing through fear is not working. What I have discovered over time is that transforming the fear always makes it easier to follow guidance.

Most of the time we avoid fear. We need to change our attitude and see that going into fear is an opportunity to grow and become freer. This will give us the necessary motivation to explore our fear.

Then there are times when it is good to explore the fear because it is our intuition guiding us to avoid something. This is why it is important to delve into it and talk to this voice of fear to get clear about it and heal it if necessary.

Here is an exercise to help you feel and resolve your fear or whatever feels out of alignment in your body.

1. Go inside and sense your body. Where is it tight? Where are you holding your breath? Where does it feel heavy or

dense? What body position would you move into if you let your body naturally move? Breathe into the area that draws you. Ask what the emotion is.

2. Ask the emotion what it is saying. For example with fear, ask what are you afraid of? What is being triggered from the past and reminding you of something? Put all your fears in the trash, from your Godself to the minus quantum particle. (page X)

3. Take your time and allow yourself to explore your sensations, emotions, memories, and everything else coming up.

4. Ask what the attitude or belief is that is creating the emotion. Is it a positive attitude that you want? If not, trash it also.

5. What is needed to heal this? If God could offer something to you, perhaps a healing statement or new belief, what would that be? (For more detailed instruction, go to Chapter 11, to the section on Reprogramming Beliefs.)

6. Notice how your body and emotions feel after receiving this new belief. Sense your body. Is your breath fuller? Is your tightness or denseness changing? Can you feel love and peace? If so, transformation is happening and you are using the right healing belief. If you don't notice these changes, go back inside and search for what belief statements make a difference when you tell them to yourself.

7. Now go back into a meditative state and ask God to give you guidance (through any of the ways we have talked about). The guidance may be the same or different as before. Sometimes the guidance is to encounter and heal our fear. If God gives you the same guidance as before (that you felt so fearful about), take this as reassurance.

8. If you still can't move forward, you need to become a detective and become curious about your process. What is coming up that doesn't feel right in your body? What

would need to happen to make you feel joyous and your heart open? Perhaps you need more information, more communication with someone, the guidance needs some adjusting, intuition is putting up red flags to be aware of, or more beliefs need to be healed by repeating the above steps. Be patient. Your process may take a while to unfold. Stay with it until you feel peaceful or joyous within your body.

9. Ask for confirmations. Sometimes God will give us the same guidance every day for a month and confirm it in many, many ways, and we'll still feel terrorized and unwilling to follow the guidance. This is a clear indication we need this inner healing work.

As an example, I went through about a month where I felt tightness in my lower left intestinal area and felt fear whenever I thought about the guidance to take Harv Ecker's Quantum Leap program. Indeed, the Leap financially terrified me! Although I tried to push through anyway, the pain never left, so I did some more detective work. I discovered many erroneous beliefs. My mind was working hard to keep me from changing and experiencing discomfort. Another belief behind this was that it was not okay to make a mistake. I realized this was a faulty belief and not a good enough reason to not follow guidance. I asked God what I needed to heal this belief. God told me I was accepted no matter what I did. Upon hearing this, I felt loved, happy, and the tightness and pain went away.

But the processing continued. Other parts of my body tightened, and I needed to share my fears with colleagues and gain more perspective. Then other fears came up, and I needed to work through these by sharing with my husband who was mirroring some of my fears as well. It took me over a month of clearing before I felt relaxed in my body and felt joy in my heart.

Resisting Guidance

Most of us, for various reasons, at times choose not to follow guidance. We get an intuition or clear message, but we brush it off or dismiss it because it means giving up something we want. Maybe the guidance is that a certain relationship is not good for you, but you want the relationship, or following the guidance will cause you to let go of money when you want to gain money at all costs.

There are many of these "lures." Most often they have to do with either desires or fears. I might not follow guidance, for example, because I want to go skiing while the guidance says to do something else. We might fear pain or want to avoid inconvenience. Sometimes we are simply being lazy.

Laziness caught me one time. I had a vision of all my sculptures having crashed on the floor of my house. I went downstairs to my art studio and glanced around, not taking much time at all. I saw nothing awry and dismissed the vision as nonsensical. As soon as I got back upstairs, I heard a loud crash. When I got downstairs, I saw ten shelves of sculptures smashed on the floor. My mistake was that I gave up too soon. I didn't persist or ask guidance more questions.

Other times we resist guidance because we want to avoid change. Yet another reason is what the Buddhists call our ignorance. In this case, ignorance comes from not seeing the whole picture because we are attached to or seeing from our small self rather than the (Higher) Self.

Not following guidance tends to have consequences, which you can see if you look for them. These may be minor consequences or very significant. One time I almost lost my house because of not following guidance about a renter; another time the distraction of desire caused me to lose a dog I'd had for a very long time. I'm sure you can identify consequences of not following guidance too.

Exploration: Not Following Guidance

- Think of a time you did not follow your guidance. Was it from fear, desire, laziness, viewing things from an ego perspective...? What lure do you think was responsible?
- How did you feel (physically, emotionally, mentally, spiritually) making this decision?
- What happened externally as a result of not following guidance?
- What happened inside of you as a result of not following guidance?
- Think of more examples, and repeat the above questions.

When I looked back over my life at the times I turned away from guidance, I saw that I gained only immediate misfortune in every situation I remembered. Not only that, I had suffered emotional, mental, physical, and spiritual inner anguish debating about whether or not to follow guidance and making the decision not to follow.

Looking at the costs of not following guidance has spurred me to follow it more, as I see it has always been in my best interest. After reflecting on the costs of not following guidance, are you inspired to follow your guidance more?

Trusting Guidance

After many, many experiences of seeing that guidance consistently supports us to increase our ability to be present with more love, courage, strength, hope, faith, truthfulness, forgiveness and fulfilling our missions, we learn to trust it. It's like any relationship where we learn to trust seeing consistent results. However, this is the key—our fear or ego bases results on keeping us comfortable, not changing, and our Higher Self or following God's guidance has results that definitely do not keep us comfortable. To trust, you have to look at your purpose for being alive on earth, as waking up to being the infinite love that you are, one with God. As Spirit became more real to me, and I learned to sense this consistent extra flow of Divine energy in my body, I came to trust it. As I followed guidance and found that it served me in spiritually growing and fulfilling my mission, I came to trust it. The more I came to trust it, the more God would challenge me with challenges in areas where I needed growth and more faith.

Speaking of not letting us down, it reminds me of a "trust fall" exercise often done in personal growth groups. A person stands in the center of a circle with eyes closed and body relatively stiff and allows their body to fall in any direction. The other participants, standing close by, catch the person and gently send them off in another direction. The person who is falling is taking a risk, but as others save them from crashing to the floor, they learn to trust the circle of fellow participants. In a similar way, when Spirit catches us again and again, we learn to trust Spirit.

My trust grew, realizing that God always made better choices for me than my ego. I was further inspired by reading Carolyn Myss' book, *Spiritual Anatomy of the Soul*. She indicated that following *Thy Will* was the spiritual lesson of the throat area, my area of weakness, and I realized that I was only committed to *Thy Will* 98%. My attention was heightened even more at the Casa saying the Lord's prayer: *Our kingdom come, thy will be done on earth, as it is in heaven.* I would watch John of God surrender his will and the Entity would come in to start the healing work. His level of surrender inspired me to surrender 100% to following *Thy Will*, Divine Love, rather than my ego fear self.

Committing 100% is about dropping our ego illusion of separateness and focusing on trusting the only presence which is God, or Divine Love. Surrendering 100% to *Thy Will* is surrendering an illusion of fear.

Why did it take me fifty-two years to surrender an illusion? How many years will it take you? Again, all I can say is God is hilarious. We are so attached to fear—what a joke! Would you rather be attached to Divine Love?

By focusing on your connection with God, it can empower you to be more daring, more in love, more true to yourself, more spontaneous, more creative, and more self-accepting. The more you trust, you learn that *whatever is* is perfect and is teaching you love.

Confronting Obstacles

Sometimes guidance comes up against obstacles. Obstacles are like an advanced course in following guidance. Obstacles may be an indication of your commitment not being 100%, or the universe testing your will and strength. Obstacles may be an indication that it's not the right timing or quite the right direction, or they may be self-created obstacles you want to find out more about. They may also be obstacles to strengthen you in your path.

This spring I went to board the airplane and handed the stewardess my ticket, but she refused to take it, saying that my ticket had been given away. But people were still boarding; I had to get on this flight or miss my class. She shut the door, saying, "This flight is full." I was mad. All flights for the next three days were full.

"Okay, God, what is up?" I asked.

"I'm putting you on the next flight in two hours; go sleep." I was tired, having been up since 2 A.M., and went to sleep. The next flight had a last minute cancellation. I got the seat next to a lady who had prayed for an alternative way to heal her cancer. God used me to heal her. God's plan was perfect. So some obstacles God creates so that we learn to trust in the perfection of what is happening.

Experiment: Confirming Guidance When There Are Obstacles

- Think of an area of your life in which you have a number of obstacles and feel stuck.
- Ask guidance if you are indeed being guided to do what you are trying to do.
- Are you committed 100%?
- Ask guidance about the meaning of this stuckness. What is your spiritual lesson?
- Ask what subconscious beliefs may be keeping the situation stuck?
- If you have fears, sadness, anger, or apprehension, express all of this and listen for God's response.
- Ask God to give you two more confirmations of this guidance. One way is to set rocks on the ground representing answers and ask God to move your body to the answer. Another way is to have your hands represent answers and have God move the hand following Divine Will.
- Go through the questions below about checking guidance. What happens in your heart? Rate the energy 1 to 10, 10 being an open heart. Does your heart and body receive more energy following this guidance than not following? Rate your energy with not following it. Does it bring you joy and love? Will the guidance bring out the best in you and others and be beneficial? Is the guidance something that God would approve of?
- Go ahead and follow this guidance after you have received confirmation.

Spiritual Teachers Point Us to God Within

Sometimes the obstacle will take the form of a teacher commitment who will challenge our trust. You develop your trust muscle by overcoming resistance. As an example, it is easy to let other people be our authority instead of God within us. One of my beloved teachers who helped me with this was Beautiful Painted Arrow. For seven years I helped lead sweat lodges and vision quests with him. One day he gave me a certain date to bring people for a vision quest. As he was talking, I saw three feet of snow and said, "No, there will be a big storm that weekend. We can't do it then." (As it turned out, this was true.)

Another friend got mad at me (for he had a different lesson) and said, "Don't argue with the teacher. He knows what's best."

"We have to change the date," I persisted. Beautiful Painted Arrow knew that my lesson was trusting God's guidance and was purposely setting me up. He was visionary and could see the future. He asked me what date we should do the quest. The date I was guided to identify was clear, with warm weather, though a bit breezy.

Another time Beautiful Painted Arrow went to a place different than what we had arranged. I saw where he was in my mind and felt compelled to confront him on it. This was difficult for me because it was the final step of disagreeing with the teacher I loved and respected. I had to become my own teacher and follow my guidance down a separate path. Beautiful Painted Arrow (Joseph Rael) had already seen this happen and told me years before that I would be ready to move on, away from him as my teacher, before I was ready to hear his knowing.

I think all great spiritual teachers point us to God within ourselves. When we understand that our essence is spiritual, being one with God and learning to trust following God becomes the goal.

Having a spiritual teacher on earth or in spirit can help motivate us to want to go inside and trust our guidance. Although some students will want to depend on the teacher, most teachers want students to depend on God. Our love and commitment for this teacher, who sets an example of following God through trusting inner guidance, inspires us to leap off cliffs into the unknown, following God also.

Thousands or perhaps millions of people feel this love/trust relationship with John of God (as The Entity), who points everyone to God within. Occasionally the Entity will instantly heal someone of cancer on stage. I've even experienced the Entity talking to me in person and being totally "off the wall" so I would stop listening to the "outer" and just trust the "inner guidance." But 99% of the time, people are sent to meditate and connect to God within, because in the larger perspective, the most important spiritual attainment is for us to be one with God. (To our usual ego selves, healing our physical bodies seems like our biggest goal, but is just a devise to awaken us to God within.)

Ask God for Help

When you notice your resistance to following God, bring this to God. Talk to God, admit your fears, and ask for help. God will often reassure you with love. Your adult self and God can reassure your inner child that you are safe.

Continue to ask for guidance to affirm that you are hearing, seeing, sensing, and being moved correctly. Ask for several confirmations to happen in the physical world that will validate Spirit's guidance.

This confirmation can be important as it is quite easy for us to distort the guidance trying to come through. Passing through the filters of our human minds with their desires, attachments, and aversions, the guidance may get tainted. There are several things that we can consider.

1. Guidance coming from Spirit is consistently loving and ultimately brings you love and joy.
2. Does it bring out the best in you, your best thoughts about yourself or others, your highest love and joy, your truth and your best actions?
3. Ask Spirit to stop you or block you if the guidance is not from Spirit, but rather from the ego.

Guidance Is Not Just for Us

It was six o'clock in the morning and I was at the airport in Brazil headed for Iguasu Falls when guidance told me to go home, so I changed my ticket and headed home two weeks early. In Denver, the sign said *light* from Salt Lake City instead of *flight* from my vantage point. I phoned Salt Lake to find out my Dad had just gone to the hospital for brain surgery.

Two hours later, I arrived at the hospital. I had been on my way to help him at 6 A.M. before he even had the fall that sent him to the hospital the following afternoon. I was grateful for the guidance and my willingness to follow. A vision told me that he had a choice to die that night at 1:30 A.M. I was sleeping in the waiting room. At 1:30, I saw Christ fill the room with light. I was in awe at the light and love that was there.

I went to see what choice my dad had made. He was alive, and a man in the next room had about twenty doctors doing emergency surgery. I knew both of them were to live and went to bed.

Again I was grateful that I followed what seemed to be off-the-wall guidance that made no sense. This was during my experiment to follow Divine Will 100% with no questions asked, just pushing through the fear. I had just arrived in Brazil four days before and the ticket was $1400.00. I had planned to be there another two weeks. It did not make any sense to my mind to fly home. I felt that my following guidance had helped my father to choose to live longer.

Now that you have remembered when following guidance made your life better, or magical, or made someone else's life better, are you inspired to follow your guidance?

> *We can't be both red and green toward God at the same time. It gets us nowhere (p.108). If your answer to this invitation (to be radically obedient) is yes, then get ready. You have not only signed up for the most incredible journey you can imagine, but you've also given God the green light to pour out His radical blessings on your life (p. 110).*
> —Radically Obedient, Radically Blessed:
> Experiencing God in Extraordinary Ways, Lysa TerKeurst

I hope that the first half of this book has helped you connect with God, the Miraculous, your guidance, and higher purpose. This is a good foundation for Part II, where we'll look at healing on the physical, mental, emotional, and spiritual levels.

Part II
Attaining Optimal Health
on All Levels

8

Discovering a Holistic Approach to Healing

For the benefit of your physical, emotional, and spiritual well-being, generate more love in your life. Each morning when you awaken, ask yourself, "How can I create more love today? How can I be open to receiving more love today?" (p. 202).

—Grow Younger, Live Longer

I would simply say quantum healing makes peace … war lies behind many diseases (p. 241).

—Quantum Healing, Exploring the Frontiers of Mind/Body Medicine, Deepak Chopra, MD.

Is your current strategy for regaining wellness effective?

My Phoenix Experience

I woke up one morning too weak and tired to get out of bed. I didn't know what was wrong. Three days before I had asked Spirit for my highest purpose. Two days before that I was feeling on top of the world, skiing powder on the steepest, most challenging runs I had ever skied. I was living heaven's paradise on earth. Now I couldn't walk.

I called the doctor; then I went to the store for a truckload of vitamins. Sound familiar? If I take thirty vitamin pills a day along with a magical chemical the doctor will give me, my body will get better. My load of vitamins cost a lot and passed instantly through my body, just like all my food. I was very sick, and my digestion was not absorbing nutrients. The vitamin tactic didn't work. Neither did the magic-pill idea. The doctor who diagnosed me with Grave's disease (hyperthyroidism) couldn't give me the magic pill for another half year. (I'll tell you about that later.)

My eight-month-old infant and I were equally vulnerable, both just trying to survive. It is nearly impossible to sleep when your heart is racing faster than it does when you are running your hardest, yet stops and leaps chaotically at the same time. I couldn't rest even though I was exhausted and was in bed eighteen hours a day.

I was aging ten times the normal rate, metabolizing six "horse meals" a day. Imagine eating four eggs, five pieces of the heaviest, heartiest bread, and half a cantaloupe, sleeping two hours and waking up starving. I ate 5,000 calories a day, including a rich pecan pie every night, and had six bowel movements a day, losing a pound a week until most of my muscles were gone and I couldn't walk. I crawled with my infant. At the age of forty, I trembled like a hundred-year-old lady and couldn't think to even write or make a telephone call to ask for help.

I had spent years in the grieving cycle described by Elisabeth Kübler-Ross. I had spent a year in shock and denial, going from a top athlete climbing 21,000-foot peaks, looking beautiful and healthy, to being unable to walk or look in a mirror without being horrified by the monstrous skeleton with protruding eyes the looked back at me. I had been a professional psychotherapist who had helped many clients, yet now was such a roller coaster of emotions that I couldn't be centered enough to talk to anyone.

I spent a year with underlying sadness facing the new body and image I didn't want, then another year in an anger, wishing I could bargain my way to health. Every once in a while, I would feel like my spirit was dying, with no hope of recovery. I'd psych myself up to walk with a cane, feel alive and healthy for a few hours, then collapse in bed exhausted for a week recovering. My friends only saw me during the psyched up hours. How could I be so sick and crawling around when they saw me on a hike? My desperation to feel healthy if only for a few moments worked short-term miracles.

No one except my doctor and child knew how sick I had really become. Zen must have been an old shaman. He would find some of my feathers from sweat lodges I did and waved them up and down over my body. This would give me more energy, and I could get us some food. There were days I trembled so bad that I thought I would faint just standing up. It was strange being so weak.

My husband did the best he could, but he could not fathom how anyone could eat a horse-sized breakfast like the one he made me and be hungry (or anywhere close to starving) before twelve hours later. The beautiful wife he had married looked like death warmed over. In his pain, shock, and denial, he became a workaholic to protect himself from total depression. In response, I became a rage-aholic, crying for the food that I was too afraid to call for after I was thrown against the wall as an infant.

I felt like I was living in a nightmare, in a *Twilight Zone* movie or the *Groundhog Day* movie where the character experiences the same thing again and again. I dreamed of waking up and climbing out of bed and out of the nightmare and of turning off the movies. Unfortunately this didn't happen.

I continued to get weaker and sicker; finally the doctor saw my blood tests. I was dying. She had her proof and gave me her best magic pill. It didn't heal me, but it bought me some time. It, like all chemicals, took away certain symptoms and created other "side effects." The side-effect of this particular magic pill was having a black cloud of depression hanging over my head.

The medication was a thyroid-blocker; it is supposed to normalize hyperthyroid conditions, which I had. If the thyroid doesn't normalize, and you continue on the medication, it can have the side-effect of making you crazy (crazier than you already have been with the condition). Thyroid blockers are therefore considered a short-term treatment if they are successful, but are not for long-term use because of these side-effects.

I was so sick that I couldn't even think. They used to put people like me (with Grave's disease) in insane asylums because our moods were like roller coasters—we were raging one minute and crying the next. Even a naturopath told me, "You can't trust yourself; you can't trust your body. You're too sick."

The only way to control Grave's disease is radiation. Three doctors told me I would die if I did not radiate. Radiation was all the medical establishment knew to do. Yet, when I heard the word *radiate*, my body would cry uncontrollably for days.

Despite being so sick I couldn't even think, an inner voice kept telling me not to do radiation. Was I going to follow my inner voice, or what the "experts" told me? If I shared this with my family, I was sure they would tie me up and take me to radiate, so I didn't tell them. Only my husband knew what I was going through.

After three years of slowly dying, one of the doctors told me I had three weeks to live unless I underwent radiation. I said, "No, Spirit says that I will heal."

"I hope you heal living and not dying," she replied.

I searched deeply inside. It was just a second, but felt like an eternity. I could find no fear of dying. "I will heal living," I told her.

What happened? I had spent my life not trusting Spirit, myself, or anyone else. How is it that when I was told I would die, I found faith and trust emerging from my center? I thought faith develops when everything goes right, "my way," not when it goes "wrong" from the personality's perspective.

I had spent three years doing everything possible with at least thirty different doctors, alternative healers, and spiritual healers. Nothing had gotten me better. I had no reason to believe it was possible for me to heal. Yet I knew beyond a doubt that I was to heal, even though I had no idea how.

I also knew that I absolutely must not go through radiation, although it was years later that I got confirmation (through the BodyScan) and learned a very important fact: that I had been overexposed to radiation as a child.

One of the things I had not realized was that the cow's milk I drank as a young child was measured by "sunshine units." This was the government's word for the nuclear radiation from the Dugway Nuclear Testing Site in Nevada that blew into Salt Lake City daily. Many people living in Salt Lake during the 1950s have thyroid problems. It was also interesting to note that the day before I collapsed in bed, I had fought with the dentist for an hour about having a dental x-ray he insisted I needed. He told me that his new machine was "low radiation," no different from getting some sunshine. Obviously even that amount of radiation was too much for me.

I didn't die, but I also didn't get well. Two months after the doctor said I had three weeks left to live, I had a talk with Spirit. "Spirit, the doctors said I was to be dead two months ago. You'd better give me a vision if I am to live."

The next day I was outside walking when all of a sudden I had a vision of the next ten years of my life. It lasted all of about three seconds, but it totally changed my life. What I saw in this vision unfolded over six years, and I experienced healing physically, mentally, emotionally, and spiritually.

I saw myself with a machine with a heavy-set man with a round face who had invented the machine and was teaching me to use it. In the vision, I was healthy and was using this machine to do healings on people. I was working with other practitioners who also use the machine. My next step was learning energy healing and spiritual healing. I saw myself help other people who were chronically ill like myself, and they got better.

When I walked inside my house, the phone was ringing. It was Ray Winfield, one of my colleagues who I hadn't talked to for a year. I told him the vision, and he identified the man I saw in the vision as Spencer Woolley, creator of the BodyScan. I called, and Spencer's first opening was a month away.

I knew I was already healed because I saw this in my vision. I had experienced visions before. Visions are not dreams to me. They are a glimpse of the future given by grace, by God. All my previous visions had become manifest.

A month later I drove to see Spencer. I asked him if he had worked with any clients with Grave's disease. He said yes. I asked him if I would heal. It is illegal to say you can heal if you are not a doctor. But I already knew the answer. Spencer was like a spiritual prophet and broke all the rules, telling me that yes, of course I would heal. I told him that if I healed, I would commit to buying this $28,000 machine. I already knew that it was time to gather my money together because I had already seen it.

In eight months I was climbing 14,000-foot peaks carrying my two-year-old son. I continued to meditate and visualize being on 21,000-foot peaks for another six years before this happened also.

There was something else interesting about my vision of Spencer and the BodyScan. I had already tried the BodyScan a year earlier and had been told it wouldn't work for me. I had not seen Spencer at that time but rather his brother. So when I had the vision, I recognized the machine but remembered it only as something that had not and would not help me. This is one of several examples where Spirit showed me something that was different than any part of my conscious mind saw as possible. As always, Spirit was right.

Developing My Healing Approach

Looking back on my life after I was well, I understood why I had gone to so many different healers. It was as though Spirit put me on a research project to experience almost every form of healing imaginable, learning the pros and cons of each method. For one year, I had tried spiritual healing. Even though I had had improvements, I was not well. I was able to walk, but my heart was still racing, I looked like a skeleton, and tired easily, I couldn't see in the sunlight, and my blood tests indicated that I was in terrible shape.

Then Spirit showed me the combination of methods that worked. What I learned was that any method that focused on the physical, mental/emotional, or spiritual by itself was not enough for the deepest healing. Healing all these levels simultaneously and achieving balance is what is most important. This is what I was instructed to create. I put several things together as a holistic approach to healing. I use psychotherapy and Chinese Energetics (www.yuenmethod.com) to address emotional and mental levels; I use the BodyScan, homeopathy, medical intuitive skills, and psychic surgery to support the physical; I teach how to connect with Spirit, how the disease fits our higher purpose, and how to use meditation to support the spiritual level. All four levels are supported in the guided meditations I lead (available on CD or Web audio—see back of book).

We begin by looking at the "commitment to healing" on all four levels. Because of my own experience, I learned how important commitment is. I felt a major part of my healing occurred when my commitment became 100%, and I released all my fear. This total commitment and the spiritual connection were two of the most important ingredients of healing, and so I incorporated them into my own work with clients.

If clients aren't at 100%, we investigate why not. Is there too much pain? What is more important than one's life? For some people, money or time is more important until their life force dwindles to a point beyond return, and their health starts to take priority. This is unfortunate because then more time and money is required. Some people find having the disease and dying easier than facing the stuff that they aren't aware of. It is sad to me that people are often so scared of finding out the hidden subconscious truths inside of them and are so scared of an unknown alternative therapy that they opt for denial and slowly dying. The well-known author and medical doctor Bernie Siegel found in his survey of clients that 100% commitment to heal was necessary for healing to happen.

When I work with peoples' diseases, I begin by calling in the awareness, presence, love, and healing of God (by whatever name the client chooses), call in Christ and the Entities of Light for myself, and call in the angels and both of our guides. I wait until I feel God's energy heighten my energy. Then I ask to be shown what Christ sees the imbalance is and how God or Christ wants to rebalance it.

I become one with Christ and then I tune into the person and the disease and become one with the disease. I feel out what the emotions are and the belief system that supports those emotions. This is often hard to do on ourselves. I have colleagues help me, because it is easier to see others than to see ourselves.

I see all the chakras and tune into the chakra that needs the healing. I get a sense of the emotions and beliefs involved. Then I tune into how old they were when it started and when the imbalance began in this life or in past lives. I tune into the primary relationship(s) that helped create it, such as mother, father, brothers, sisters, other relatives, friends, coworkers, bosses or however. All sorts of information is given to me. I am shown what the healing words and emotions need to be and what happens when this is provided to the imbalanced area. Then we implement this solution physically so the client feels the difference in their body and knows it is working.

I will have to explain that I work with clients who have physical imbalances, are in pain, and may have chronic conditions that are life-threatening. I love these clients because they are more motivated to heal quickly. We don't have to spend a month developing trust, as in traditional therapy. They trust me or they wouldn't work with me for even the first session. Also unlike traditional therapy, I don't spend six months helping them dig up the issues to resolve them. When the doctor gave me three weeks to live, God gave me three weeks to heal deep emotional wounds that hadn't gotten healed in twenty years of psychotherapy. That's why I like this system.

The client basically re-parents themselves (with God's help) and takes responsibility to commit to do healing work a half hour a day. No therapist can do this amount of therapy as fast as clients who are diligently working on themselves.

Clients who are committed to this work (all of my clients) do their homework because I show them through their own experience the difference made by ten minutes of homework. I also show them what difference their homework will make as charted by the BodyScan, which shows them a graph of their energy in relationship to their disease. (See page 106 for an introduction to this tool.) My message to them is that the work they do at home is more important than what happens in my office.

All of my clients are given homework using a method described in this book that involves utilizing an unconditionally loving figure to give corrective messages and then practice receiving those messages. (See page X.)

In addition to what I have just described, I use the BodyScan, homeopathy, Chinese Energetics, and psychic surgery, all of which I include in the next chapter. Using all of these techniques, the four levels—physical, mental, emotional, and spiritual—are all supported.

9

Body-Centered Healing

Spencer Woolley, developer of the Phazx BodyScan, taught and modeled like a saint, that love has the power to heal the world. "To be a conscious, self-actualized person means to break free from the limits of self by surrendering self-will to divine will. It means to be aware of the body as an expression of the spirit, a physical carrier of consciousness. It means to live life with love, honor and forgiveness.... Let the physical world and your body be your teachers. Align them with the spirit—and don't skip school."

Do you want to heal the sources or to cover up symptoms?

When we are sick, all we want is to heal our physical bodies as quickly as possible. Hopefully, you now know that the physical level is rarely the source to be healed. If you want healing, it is only possible by balancing the spiritual, mental and emotional levels also. Check in with yourself (or a therapist) to find out if you are in alignment with feeling deserving, ready, able, and committed to healing while remaining unattached and yet expecting healing to happen (Yuen Method).

In this chapter, we'll look at a number of healing modalities as well as the cause of disease.

Bioenergetic Medicine

Bioenergetic medicine views people (and animals) as energetic beings. It is based on Einstein's principles, Chinese

Medicine, and Spiritist understandings which assert that body functions are based on energy. Chemical reactions are secondary and take place because of energy. (Western allopathic medicine, in contrast, asserts that chemical reactions are the primary determinant of body functioning.)

Because we are energetic beings, imbalances show up energetically years before they manifest physically. Do you realize what this means? This means that an instrument such as the Phazx BodyScan, other bioenergetic machines, and medical intuitive readings can pick up energy imbalances, up to eight years ahead of the time that they manifest as disease states. This means that diseases can energetically be healed while they are still imbalanced energy states. In other words, diseases can be prevented.

Bioenergetic medicine uses twenty Chinese meridian systems to measure your body's flow of energy and communication, plus methods like the Phazx BodyScan described below.

With bioenergetic medicine, your body can tell us what level (the physical, mental/emotional, or spiritual) is important to work on and the impact of that level. Your body can be asked how much stress any disease is, and how much that will be reduced by using homeopathy, doing emotional homework, spiritual alignment, and so on. My Phazx BodyScan machine scientifically confirms to people what their body is telling them. It also confirms scientifically all the healing work God does through me. Clients usually *see* their body's healing. Bioenergetic medicine is paving the way of the future. It can be used to assist doctors in every way, especially testing chemicals before potential allergic responses or side-effects!

I found bioenergetic medicine and homeopathy (explained below) to be the most effective healing tools available, especially when people are in phases 4, 5, and 6 of the "phases of health" described next.

The Phases of Health

A homotoxicology chart, developed by Hans Heinrich Reckeweg, M.D., a medical doctor who became a homeopath, analyzes toxic build-up and disease development in his book, *Homotoxicology: Illness and Healing through Anti-homotoxic Therapy*. He developed this theory to integrate the medical sciences with principles of homeopathy.

In the first phase of health, the body naturally eliminates toxins as fast as they enter the body by sweating, urinating, and defecating. In the second phase, more toxins enter than the body can eliminate, so it needs to use vomiting, or mucous (such as bacteria in pneumonia) to get rid of toxins. In the third phase, additional toxins are deposited in the joints (e.g. causing arthritis) which the lymph has to work extra hard to eliminate. These three phases have "uncomfortable symptoms" but are considered in the range of health, since the body has the energy to heal itself by eliminating the toxins.

The next three phases are when the body has given up on getting rid of the toxins. It no longer has the ability to heal itself. Instead it manages the toxins by putting them in a weak organ, by sacrificing the weak organ, or by encapsulating the toxins in a tumor or cancer to save the heart and the rest of the body functions. These phases are dangerous, because they often lack the annoying symptoms, but the body is increasingly exhausted. My thyroid was filled with radiation and heavy metal poisoning in the fourth phase, became degenerated in the fifth phase, and would have developed cancer in the sixth phase.

Because of my goal of optimal health, I added three phases. I felt there was something better than just maintaining health and that was achieving optimal health. In these three phases, I describe moving toward an ideal state. Physically this involves having optimal energy and strength, energy reserves, needing less sleep, and being free of all symptoms of disease. Emotionally, one is filled with unconditional love, joy, peace, and gratitude. Mentally, there is a lack of judgments and a focus on positive beliefs, blessings, and forgiveness. Spiritually, there is a feeling of being one with Spirit and all that is.

The Phazx BodyScan

Using the Phazx BodyScan, one can determine which of the above phases of health a person is in.

The Phazx BodyScan, developed by Spencer Woolley (and Bill Nelson), is based on the premise that everything has a vibrational pattern. It can create these patterns and send them through the body to see how the body reacts. Simply said, a vibration of a potential stressor (e.g. a bacteria) is energetically sent through you, and you send the computer a message that there is no stress, no resistance, no problem, or you short-circuit and say you are stressed and need help. You can then test a possible treatment: so for example, a bottle of bacteria homeopathy is given to you to see if you light up and flow or continue to be in distress. Remedies can be tested this way and thus known to work energetically before you buy them.

The Phazx BodyScan test analyzes 5 to 10,000 possible body stressors. (It does all this in about ten minutes.) Those that most stress the body can be introduced to the system so that the body can learn how to effectively resolve them.

Because I didn't want to be dependent on a machine and wanted to do healings anytime, anywhere, I became a medical intuitive and integrated the BodyScan's information into my being. When I do BodyScan readings on people, I simultaneously am doing medical intuitive readings as well and getting other information.

The BodyScan and Medical intuitive readings often give a different sense of a problem than objective tests, such as blood tests. Here is an example. Let's say your thyroid may show up on these subjective and energetic methods as quite imbalanced and be calling for help. In contrast, a blood test may not show an imbalance because either the imbalance is still energetic or the norms for the test are so wide that you fall into the normal range, but it is not normal and certainly not optimal for you.

It works the other direction too. You energetically heal before the physical heals, so energetically you may be showing balance and healing when a more objective physical measure such as a blood test is still lagging behind. It is good to get medical intuitive assessments and BodyScan readings that ask your body how it feels it is doing.

After checking all of your major meridians, body systems, organs, hormones, vitamins, minerals, and pathogens such as bacteria, virus, molds, parasites, heavy metals, and allergies, I look for a remedy that will help you. These remedies are considered homeopathic (see below), but may also include flower essences, which help heal the emotional levels.

I use homeopathy to help people heal on the physical level whether I am doing the BodyScan or medical intuitive readings. This homeopathic remedy is a combination of many supportive vibrations, which I'll explain more in the next section. By the end of the session, I check to make sure that all your meridians, organs, and systems balance and have flowing communication so necessary for good health.

Homeopathy

Homeopathy is based on taking the most minute amount of a substance which acts as a messenger to stimulate the body to heal itself. (This is in contrast with allopathic medicines which take over for the body and do not strengthen the body's own defense.)

In homeopathy, the body uses the message, re-patterns itself, and becomes stronger and more resilient. Sometimes the homeopathic remedy will exaggerate a symptom first before healing it. That's not so popular in our American culture, which wants a quick fix. On the other hand, unlike pharmaceutical drugs that you may continue taking for years, a homeopathic remedy is used by the body to create a change and resolve the problem, and then you stop taking the remedy.

Within four weeks, your body gets stronger using whatever the message of the homeopathic remedy is and heals itself at that level. It is like tuning up a symphony. When you tune the violins (or heart), then you may be able to hear that the violas (or lungs) now need tuning. Healing is a process of tuning all four levels. You may need a different remedy to resolve a different problem or a different level.

Remedies come in different strengths, depending on how distilled the substance has become. It can become so distilled that no substance is detectable, but the imprint or vibrational pattern of the substance is still there. (This is sometimes referred to as a "light imprint.") The more refined this substance has become, the deeper it can go into the cells. These imprints show the body how it can and should be functioning.

In this type of homeopathy, I am trying to give the body something to model itself after. So, for example, if the heart needs help functioning, I want to give it instruction on what optimal heart functioning is like. I do this by providing a "light imprint" of healthy heart.

Also, I abide by the theory that the body is able to assimilate many homeopathic remedies at a time, and so I use "combination" remedies. There may be as many as 100 different homeopathics within one bottle.

When Samuel Hahnemann developed homeopathic remedies in the early 1800s, our lives were simpler and the number of stressors was much smaller. Simple constitutional homeopathic remedies provided healing for the majority of people. In my experience of working with three top classical homeopathic doctors for a year using one homeopathic remedy at a time, this was woefully inadequate. My situation was far too complex for one homeopathic remedy to produce the needed changes.

This "classical homeopathy" works like an inoculation where the body learns to address something that is a threat to it. So, for example, if you are bitten by a snake, you give the body a tiny dose of the poison. I use these constitutional remedies for dealing with *miasms*, which are genetic weaknesses considered to go back to the beginnings of humankind. According to constitutional theory there are a small number of conditions that began all of our diseases. Each one of these (miasms) has associated mental, emotional, and spiritual issues. In the work I'm doing, people work through a series of miasms, resolving issues on all four levels.

Spencer Woolley, the founder of the BodyScan, who was trained as a classical homeopathic practitioner, did not find the constitutional remedies to be adequate for many of his clients. He developed the BodyScan to use both constitutional (classical) homeopathic remedies and combination ("polycrest") homeopathic remedies, which include some that tell the organs how to be healthy (as described above). I use both of these.

My experience is that homeopathics can also be created using Spirit. If I am traveling in foreign countries, Spirit will create the homeopathic remedy by putting in all the vibrations that are needed for healing into water to create a remedy. Also when Christ does a healing through me, I am shown the healed body. When the person takes the remedy, they are aligning with the blueprint of health that Christ showed me. All is possible with God, and this is a good illustration.

The next major form of physical healing is having God, Christ, the Entities of Light, or the angels do psychic surgery. I have found this to be extremely effective with holistic work on all the other levels being done at the same time.

Psychic Surgery

The psychic surgery I have experienced has been much easier on my body than physical surgery. Psychic surgery is also known as *invisible* or *spiritual surgery*.

I had a client who was told by doctors on separate occasions that he needed a heart valve replacement, a leaky artery fixed, and his arteries cleaned out. He instantly healed each of these with psychic surgery and had the doctors confirm this days later. I had a lady with uterine cancer go in for the operation two weeks after psychic surgery and homeopathy, only to find out the cancer was gone. Another client had psychic surgery on numerous twenty-year-old breast cysts. I told her to not look for three days and then report back to me. They were all gone.

I can't describe how others do psychic surgery, but this is the process that happens for me. I feel a strong universal energy coming down through my head, out my third eye, heart, and hands. As this happens, I psychically watch Christ, Mary, angels, and guides go in and perform the psychic surgery. I watch the intervention in close-up detail within the organs and systems. The surgery may be stopped because I am told that there is a block emotionally, mentally, or spiritually that needs clearing first. After we use Chinese Energetics (next chapter) or psychotherapeutic work to clear the blocks, the psychic surgery is completed. The physical results may be instantaneous or a process.

My job is to connect with God, help you to connect with God, have my love and heart open to your heart, and allow the universal energy of Divine Love to flow through us and perform the psychic surgery. Ultimately, it is the Divine that is doing the healing, and each person's receptivity is critical.

I love instant results, so I do all I can to check for any blocks. I am not in control of your life lessons, process, or interaction with God, so I also have to trust the process whatever it is. I am not a doctor. I don't cure, heal, diagnose, or prescribe. I leave this to your body wisdom and God. In all that I do, I am tuning into the wisdom of your body and into God to get answers. Legally it is always advised that you consult your doctor and do not replace this for medical treatment unless a doctor tells you. As a minister, I tell people to ask God for guidance.

Diet

A healthy diet is another important aspect of tuning up the symphony within your body. Unfortunately for people focusing on diet, it is only a portion of the picture. For two years I followed a strict Candida diet to correct my Candida and acid issues. I made more headway with changing my pH in fifteen seconds with a half-hour Yuen Method session than with diet. This is why I emphasize balancing all the levels and doing the best you can while enjoying your life.

It makes sense to eat as much fresh fruits and vegetables as you can. This helps to mineralize and alkalize your body. I've noticed almost all of my clients with chronic conditions all have an over-acid body which is the result of negative thoughts, feeling separate from God, having unresolved emotions of fear, anger, and sadness and eating acid-producing food. Sugar, caffeine, alcohol, chocolate, and meat are acidic. An overuse of these substances often has a mental, emotional, or spiritual origin.

The major ways to alkalize your body are to think positive thoughts; feel one with God; focus on feeling love, joy, and peace; and forgive yourself and others. Drink filtered or bottled water, eight or more cups of it, depending on your weight and activity level. Bless all you eat with light, love, and gratitude, and affirm that it will be 100% nourishing to your body. In addition to foods that alkalize the body, take *Trace Mineral Concentrates*™, which is a concentrated form made of Great Salt Lake minerals. It is the cheapest, best, most natural alkalizer I know. Drink spirulina or take blue-green algae. Buy wheat grass tablets or, even better, buy a tray of wheat grass. Get out your blender, add a handful of grass, ½ cup of water, push the button, and then strain this through a net, a sock, or a painter's screen, and drink it. Use natural evaporated sea salt or Celtic salt instead of processed salt which causes high blood pressure and heart problems. Natural salts actually feed the body, especially the heart, which is a muscle and has to have minerals.

Eat as simply, fresh, and naturally as possible. When food is processed or cooked with temperatures over 120 degrees, it is acidified. Ideally eat foods raw or cook stir-fried like the Chinese do, just enough to heat the outside and keep the inside of the vegetable low heat.

Fresh produce is best and cheapest, so resist canned, frozen, and dried foods when possible. Choose whole grains over processed pastas and breads. Grains and milk are basically neutral. Meats are acidic, but if your diet has a lot of fruits and vegetables, this balances out. I find most people can use Bragg's Liquid Amino's™ for supporting muscles, and flax seed oil for supporting nerves, and olive oil as a basic oil of choice.

The BodyScan and medical intuitive reading tell us if there are any deficiencies in the diet or allergies to foods or chemicals. Foods causing allergies can be eliminated and/or de-allergized by finding and correcting the source of the problem.

There are fabulous books on diets for each body type that are fun if you want to get into this type of detail. But, I must emphasize that it is more about having the quality of love in your life than getting your diet "right." If dropping coffee is going to be super stressful, then bless your coffee to neutralize the acid. Homeopathic doctors will think I am off my rocker when I say that I program clients to take homeopathy with their coffee. If you are willing to stop coffee, it's true that not drinking battery acid every day will create a more alkaline body. Eating the "perfect" diet and being highly anxious all day may cause more acid than coffee or sugar.

I think it is important to accept clients wherever they are at and work with them at their level of willingness. God always finds a way to creatively work with anyone and shows me how to stretch my imagination. I work with doctors, their prescribed chemicals, radiation, and homeopathy. Everyone has their own path and needs to respect it.

Exercise

Exercise is a basic necessity of good health. It helps clean most of the body systems, especially the lymph system, which is one of our most important ways of detoxing. Exercise also keeps us happy when it is energetic and sustained through producing endorphins, "pleasure chemicals" in our brains.

During my healing, I pushed myself and went beyond my capacity to maintain my strength; this led to relapses sending me to bed two and three days at a time. (This is normal with chronic fatigue.) I don't want you to over-do it and lose ground, so I suggest slowly building up an exercise regime. It is easy to exercise by doing isometrics just lying down or sitting. Tensing your muscles and holding a few seconds can be an effective work-out. Most people hate to exercise, because it is a lot of work when you don't feel well. Brainstorm how to have fun doing some sort of exercise with friends. There is usually some inspiring solution that can motivate the most resistant person to exercise.

I'll have to say that one of the things that kept my Spirit alive was exercising in nature. Being outside helped me feel whole, and I remembered being healthy. Even though I would be in bed for days recovering from my outing, my Spirit tasted health. One of the most important ways to heal the body is to feel healthy, to see yourself as healthy, to affirm that you are healthy in every way.

IO

Healing Emotional Patterns

Happiness is a sign that we have accepted God's will (p. 239).
—*A Return to Love: Reflections on
the Principles of* A Course in Miracles.

*Do you want more happiness and less
physical imbalances?*

My guess is that 85% of the time, emotions are the cause
of physical disease. I can think of many examples from my
life, but let me share some of my client's stories instead.

Examples of Emotional Healings
That Resolved Physical Symptoms

I worked with a woman who had chronic sore throats.
Within fifteen minutes of starting our work, her pain was
gone and the redness reduced. When I became her sore
throat, I saw her unable to speak her truth and feel supported
and heard by her husband.

I had her tune into her inner child who felt sad and angry about not being heard and afraid to speak. Fortunately,
she was able to sense her throat and acknowledge this truth
inside of her. I tuned into what the inner kid needed to hear
in order to heal. The words were, "I love you. I love supporting you and taking care of you. I want to listen to you.
You are safe to speak. Please tell me everything you would

like to say." She breathed in love and found where this truth was inside of her throat. She breathed in more love and kept expanding this love. Then she said, "I feel supported and cared about" and felt this within her. "I feel heard. I feel safe to speak."

As she felt this, her sore throat went away. For homework, I gave her an assignment of going back and forth between this loving voice and her inner child to practice a half-hour a day and whenever her throat began to get sore.

Her throat became sore the next fight she had with her husband, but when she did the homework, it went away. The more she practiced the homework, the more her relationship with her husband transformed. She began to feel supported and heard by him and opened up to having this experience happen.

I had an elderly lady who had uterine cancer become aware of her emotional loneliness and wanting her friends to give her love and attention. We had her feel loved by God and Mary, but she didn't continue this homework. I asked Christ to do psychic surgery and saw Christ remove her tumor. I gave her homeopathy for the cancer. Two weeks later when she went to the surgery, the cancer was gone. The doctors, however, convinced this 88-year-old woman to let them take out all her female organs to prevent any future possible cancer. She agreed, which fit her need to receive love from her friends who took care of her. This is an interesting case where the medical intervention filled an emotional need.

An elderly man with Huntington's disease was hardly able to talk or understand others talking to him. We worked on releasing his embarrassment and guilt about not being enough. He replaced this with God's love and loving himself as well as receiving love on a continuous, 24-hour-a-day basis from his angelic wife.

I watched Christ do many psychic surgeries on him, as well as giving him homeopathy for a year. I also took his photo to John of God. Because he loved his pharmaceutical pills so much, I reprogrammed him (according to Chinese Energetics) so that the pills would have 100% healing effects on him with no negative effects, and cleared his nervous system using this same system.

Today he talks normally to everyone, understands everyone, is reading academic scientific books that I don't understand, and instead of sleeping most of the day is up until midnight reading every night. He is off oxygen most of the time and traveled on an airplane for the first time in five years to visit John of God in Atlanta.

His wife had chronic fatigue. After doing emotional work that allowed her to accept that her husband was in the hands of God, in essence, *letting go and letting God*, she had major breakthroughs and got her life back.

I have found that working with the animals in the chakras, as explained below, is effective in healing symptoms. I had a client who was a very accomplished professional woman who was unable to get pregnant. She thought she had resolved any issue that could be interfering, yet when I had her go into the chakras and encounter the animals there, the animals were all babies. She acknowledged that she had, in fact, always felt very young, despite her accomplishments. This woman's father had died when she was still a girl and she had always been looking for a father. In our work, she was able to find a mature part of her that could re-parent this young aspect. This part of her could then grow up, which was reflected by the animals in the second chakra becoming adult animals that were ready to welcome a baby. After this, she conceived, and she recently delivered a healthy baby. This work is very powerful. Sometimes our intellect can fool us. We may be very sophisticated functioning in the world but emotionally still quite immature. The chakra work is one of the easiest ways I know to both see what is going on and to change it.

Exploring the Chakras

I find that the chakra centers reflect the emotional issues of our inner children as well as our subconscious beliefs. When people come in with diseases, I see and feel the subconscious two-year-old that is creating the disease, crying for help, and most likely creating discomfort in the person's life. The two-year-old has all sorts of wounding from past lives, being in the womb, being born, and just living life. For example, you probably felt scared when the doctor grabbed you, hung you upside down, and hit you on the butt. For the rest of your life, there is fear and the belief that people hurt you.

The following is a fun process of using the inner animals and energy or chakra centers to discover these inner beliefs. The chakra energies and animals never lie, so I like looking at them—especially when a person doesn't think their disease has anything to do with mental beliefs or emotions.

In this exploration, you will playfully engage your inner animals to find these hidden emotions and attitudes. You'll want to work from as receptive a state as possible and try to keep your conscious mind out of it. Try to approach this as a treasure hunt into the mystery of yourself. Whatever comes up is the greatest gift that your body can give to you. Wisdom so often resides in our more "primitive" ways of knowing. You'll also want paper and pencil or colored pens to record your experience. You can plan to explore one chakra at a sitting or several. I suggest you plan on about 15-30 minutes for each chakra if you do all the steps.

In the latter part of the process with each chakra, the God-Self will say something to the small self. (These are in italics.) The really critical piece is the small self being able to fully take this in God's love, all the way through the chakra and the body. There is a phrase to affirm this reality, and it is essential to focus inwardly as you say this.

Root Chakra

1. When you're ready, relax and tune into your root chakra. Sense your legs and genital area, feel any emotions, notice any thoughts. Even touch your legs to tune in better.
2. Allow an animal to emerge that represents your energy in this area of your body.
3. Now feel your emotions and watch any attitudes emerge as you investigate who you are as this animal. You may have to imagine there are also other animals to give you a sense of safety, being wanted, and wanting to be here. Take five minutes to explore your animal.
4. As this animal, I'd like you to sense how safe you feel in the world. Sense how much you feel wanted. Sense how much you want to be here on earth.
5. Do a quick sketch or write a description of yourself as this animal. You can draw a representative sketch or something that simply expresses the energy of the animal.
6. Now go in and talk to this inner animal. Have Mother or Father God or some more mature aspect of yourself talk to it, repeating the following words or your own words. Tell this animal that you (as God or whichever of these you choose) absolutely want it.
7. Notice if this feels uncomfortable in any way. Whenever I say a phrase and your body gets tense, or you feel scared, sad, or angry, or your mind goes "that's not true," pay attention, open your eyes, express this to whoever it belongs to. Release these emotions and beliefs. These are indications that your subconscious, your inner two-year-old has a different belief.
8. You may even want to jot down on paper a key word. For example, if it feels uncomfortable to hear that you are absolutely wanted, then on some level your inner self feels unwanted. Write down *unwanted*.

9. The exercise below is something for you to focus on as homework for a month. I am taking you through this exercise to play with where hidden beliefs and emotions keep you from your oneness with Mother/Father God. Use this as an opportunity to be aware of your response. There is no judgment, only gratitude for the truth emerging in a playful way. Whatever truth arises, see it as your inner two-year-old's way of surviving. These ways are probably not necessary anymore, and with this new awareness you are free to have new choices. Isn't this great! Now back to the exercise.

10. (Again have Father or Mother God repeat, *We want you.*) Feel this message of being wanted and breathe this into your root chakra. See your animal. Speak from your animal, saying, "I feel wanted."

11. Let this call and response pattern continue. (I will put the *call* part in italics and the *response* in quotation marks.) *Know that we (Father God, Mother God, and your self) are always here keeping you safe and protected.* "I feel safe and protected."

12. *We love you.* Say, "I feel loved."

13. Now watch your animal and see if it transforms into a new animal. There may be several such transformations. Just keep feeling Mother/Father God in your hands as love (your hands may get hot) and watch how your animal evolves for the next three minutes.

14. Draw your final animal when you feel finished.

Abdominal Chakra

Now we will tune into the abdominal animal.

1. See your inner animal.

2. Now allow yourself to explore as this animal for five minutes and learn more about who you are. If you wish, make a drawing to remember this animal.

3. As this animal, feel how it is to be male or female. Notice how it feels to be sensual, how loved you are, how connected to others and God you feel. Notice how much you trust that you are cared about and will be taken care of; feel how much you trust yourself.

4. Now put your hands below your belly button on the second chakra. Once more as Father/Mother God and/or your full self and say, *We love you with all our hearts.* Breathe this in and feel it. Respond as the animal with "I feel totally loved." If there is any objection, open your eyes, express yourself to whom it applied to and then repeat the process. Tell this inner animal, *We are always here with you.* If it feels right, respond as the animal with "I feel connected with you." *We are always taking loving care of you.* From the animal, "I feel taken care of by everyone." *You can trust that we will always be here loving and taking care of you.* "I trust I am taken care of." *We trust that you know what you need and honor your needs.* "I trust myself and feel I am honored trusting myself."

5. Shut your eyes and watch this animal transform into a new animal.

6. Take a minute to draw this.

Solar Plexus Chakra

We are up to the third chakra. Put your hands above your diaphragm area. We'll go through much the same procedure.

1. Look inside and see which animal appears.

2. Take five minutes to explore being this animal.

3. As this animal, notice how much you feel guided and supported. Feel how much you **are** in control or how controlled you are.

4. Make a drawing to express the feeling of the animal or its energy.

5. Put your hands on your solar plexus and be Mother/Father God saying, *We treasure you. You are the most important part of us.* Let the animal respond, "I feel treasured. I feel important." *We are always here guiding you.* "I feel guided." *We are always here supporting you and applauding whatever you are doing.* "I feel supported and applauded." *We support you and empower you to be true to yourself.* "I feel supported to be myself." *We support you to feel in control.* "I feel in control."

6. Shut your eyes and watch as your solar plexus animal changes.

7. Make a quick sketch that captures what animal you are left with.

Heart Chakra

1. Tune into the animal in your heart.

2. Now allow yourself to explore being this animal for five minutes.

3. As this animal, notice how unconditionally loved you feel and how safe you feel to unconditionally love.

4. Make a quick sketch which reflects what you've seen so far.

5. Put your hands on your heart as Mother/Father God and say, *We unconditionally love you. You are safe to let in all our love.* "I feel safe feeling unconditionally loved." *You are safe to express all your love.* "I feel safe expressing all my love."

6. Allow the animal to transform.

7. Draw a picture that reminds you of this new energy.

Throat Chakra

1. See your throat animal.

2. Take five minutes to discover who you are as this animal.

3. As this animal, notice how much you feel heard and listened to through your life. Notice how safe you feel to

express all your emotions and thoughts. Notice how safe you feel listening to others and being true to yourself.
4. Make a quick sketch.
5. Let's talk to this animal and part of your body. Hold your hands on your throat and as Mother/Father God say, *We love to hear what you say and how you feel. No matter what it is, please tell us.* "I feel safe sharing my emotions and thoughts. I feel heard." We support you listening to others and remaining true to yourself. I feel able to listen to others and remain true to myself.
6. Allow the animal to transform.
7. Draw a picture that reminds you of this new energy.

Third Eye Chakra

1. See what animal is alive in this chakra.
2. Take five minutes to really experience what you feel like as this animal.
3. As this animal, notice how much eagerness you have to see into the future and to dream. Notice how much you believe in your dreams and visions of the future. How much do you feel others believe in your dreams?
4. Let's talk to this animal. Put your hands on your third eye and as Mother/Father God say, *Your dreams are God coming through you. We encourage your dreams, we love your dreams, we believe in your dreams, and we totally support your dreams.* "I feel encouraged to dream. I feel supported to dream. I feel my dreams are important. I believe in my dreams. I feel others believe in my dreams."
5. Tune into your animal and watch what happens.
6. Sketch this animal.

Crown Chakra

1. Go to the top of your head and allow yourself to see this animal.
2. Explore being this animal for five minutes.

3. Sketch this animal.
4. As this animal, notice how much you are connected with Mother/Father God. Feel your oneness with the universal energy.
5. Put your hands on top of your head and as Mother/Father God say, *You are our essence.* "I feel my essence is God." *You are one with us.* "I feel one with God." *You are perfect in our eyes.* "I feel perfect." *We approve of all of you.* "I feel you approve of me. I approve of myself." *We appreciate everything you are, do, and say.* "I feel appreciated for being myself and all I do and say."
6. Watch how your animal changes.
7. Sketch this new manifestation.

In working with this exercise, I find that the animals in blocked chakras are small, immature, scared, protected types. They become stronger or even change into a stronger animal after taking in the healing messages. If a person's chakra energy is balanced, the animal will tend to already be strong and mature.

We will focus in on additional themes associated with the chakras in the next chapter when we look at core beliefs.

Strangled by Fear

Several important teachers have said that there are basically two emotions: love and fear. In love, we are one with spirit; in fear, we feel separate. Dealing with fear is an important skill for those wanting to heal and be whole.

Yuen Method (www.yuenmethod.com) is a healing system created by Dr. Kam Yuen. He understood how important it is to not have fear clouding the system. When fear is present, we can't receive healing or true guidance from God. We also attract to us what we fear. In his system, one of Dr. Kam Yuen's primary mechanisms for working with fear is to become aware of it by exaggerating it. Here is an example of his using this with me.

I had previously had some dental problems that I thought I had neutralized my fears about. When Kam got me up on stage for a demonstration, the first thing he asked was, "How would you feel if all your teeth fell out?"

I said that I would feel that I was dying.

"How would I feel about dying at this moment?" Kam asked. (He has a knack at tapping into our horror.) So I threw everything in the trash that bothered me about dying and losing all my teeth. I revisited how I felt about dying and found I had no charge, I was okay, therefore open to God guiding me again. In another session on my protruding eyes, the first thing he asked was, "How would you feel being hung to death with your eyes popping out?" All summer long, my son had kept showing me how trout eyes pop out when you squish their neck. After my hour-long session with Kam, my eyes, which were about 30% normal became 90% normal. The $400 session with Kam saved me the $13,000 it would cost to do physical surgery as well as a lot of pain. Everyone who saw me called it miraculous as well.

So one way to find your fears is to simply exaggerate your symptom and notice if there is fear. If you need help, ask any kid to help you or a Yuen Method therapist or take my classes (page X) or Dr. Yuen's classes. Ask how many stressors contribute to this fear. There may be millions of such fears in the body. Mentally, send them into the trash. Feel to see if you are still as bothered by the fear.

In order to heal, we need to release our fears. Using the Yuen Method, I help the person sense universal love energy, heaven to earth to heaven, which also strengthens the body, reprograms their front and back spinal meridians (conceptual and governing channels) and their central nervous system to release millions of fears on the conscious and subconscious levels, including fears that have been passed through generations. My eyes reexperienced fear when my son and I were playing and his fist hit my eyes. They popped back out with the fear. I sent the fear to the trash and realized I had not done the emotional homework to maintain the healing and reduce unknown triggers of fear. My eyes instantly receded again.

Loving What Is

In order to heal, we need to expect to heal but not to be attached to healing. Although this seems like a contradiction, fears and attachments stop the universal energy. Attachment to healing means that we are not able to accept ourselves the way we are. Before Kam worked on my eyes, I practiced the following technique for loving a disease or symptom.

- Think of your disease or a symptom of your disease or any part of your body that you don't like. Use the following as a model.
  Say, "I unconditionally love my _____" (symptom).
- Is this true? How do you feel about the symptom? (e.g. anger, frustration, sadness). Feel it in your body.
- Now love this feeling, affirming. "I unconditionally love my ____ (emotion)."
- How do you feel about loving this emotion? What new emotion arises? Say, "I unconditionally love my _____" (emotion).
- Repeat until you get to peace.
- Now go back to "I unconditionally love my _____" (symptom) and let a new feeling arise.
- Go through the same process with it.
- Continue extending love to yourself for feeling the various emotions you feel about your symptom until you come to a point of being able to read "I unconditionally

love my _____" (symptom) and feel unconditional love and peace.

To accept how we truly feel about a situation frees us up. This lets the energy flow again. When we don't love and accept how we are, we are not free to change.

Spend at least a half hour doing this exercise and repeat it on every aspect of your disease.

I did this process with my popped-out eyes. I spent an hour sobbing with every line and cleared out a lot of the feelings. My acceptance grew to the point where, when little children would bug out their eyes at me, I didn't react any longer (I used to be very upset).

I find it useful to think of symptoms as "little children asking for help." Our bodies create symptoms and disease to get our attention. When hurt children come to you, do you help them better by loving them or by telling them to go away because you hate them? Symptoms are like hurt children; they definitely will not go away if you say that you hate them. They will rebel and get your attention in mischievous ways.

As difficult as it is to minister to the hurt child within us, we must attend to this with love and acceptance. Only then will the symptom get the attention it needs. The result is that the symptom will no longer need to exist. Practice the unconditional love exercise with total devotion to accepting yourself as you are. Love is the key to healing and attaining optimal health.

II

Transforming Negative Core Beliefs

The dream you are living is your creation. It is your perception of reality that you can change anytime. You have the power to create hell and you have the power to create heaven.... Why not use your mind, your imagination, and your emotions to dream heaven?... What you will see is love coming out of the trees, love coming out of the sky, love coming out of the light. You will perceive love from everything around you. This is the state of bliss. You perceive love directly from everything, including yourself and other humans. Even when humans are sad or angry, behind these feelings you can see that they are also sending love (pp. 123–4).

The Four Agreements, Don Miguel Ruiz.

What dream is running your life?

As you are learning, our subconscious beliefs normally run us, even though we are not aware of them. It is as if we have old videos running our minds and bodies. When we become aware, we can choose to replace these videos with new, more appropriate videos.

For example, in my own life, the times I went to put on healing events, I would lose the capacity of all of my communication systems. Suddenly, three or four phones would break, fax machines and computers would stop working, even my palm pilot had an irretrievable meltdown. I discovered that on a subconscious level I had a belief that the world (on which I had projected my parental attitudes) didn't want to know the real me and didn't want to connect with me. This brought up fear and a belief that I couldn't connect with them. And true to this belief, I couldn't connect! Consciously I had no idea that this was happening until I deeply investigated the situation. Each time this has happened the belief was slightly different, and so the wording for healing the belief also had to be different. Healing these deep beliefs is a process. As our beliefs are healed, our perceptions of the world change.

I've seen instant manifestation of my anger and negative attitudes bring about an unexpected storm and thirty-foot waves big enough to swallow a houseboat on Lake Powell. When I looked into the blackness of the curling wave, I had a deep realization that my unconscious negative thoughts could and would kill me if I didn't learn to be aware of them. This motivated me to live in an ashram for a year and learn other forms of meditation as well as to become a psychotherapist. This example clearly shows how our internal beliefs (positive or negative) create the external reality that we perceive.

Another powerful example was my client who had the belief that people hurt her. She had been walking down a road in Denver and hit by a bullet, as well as hit by a stray bullet riding in a bus, and by a stray bullet that went through a hotel wall from the next room, and yet another time—this was four times! Unfortunately she chose to blame these experiences as strange coincidences that had nothing to do with her and would not consider the homework I gave her. She also would not believe that her illness had anything to do the victim part of her that wanted help healing.

The good news is that you can change beliefs (and outcomes) and can reprogram yourself at the cellular level using methods in this book that I find are much more effective than affirmations. In the exercises in this chapter, we'll bring in as much help as possible in healing the beliefs that so contribute to our suffering.

Core Beliefs

Although there are an infinite number of beliefs we hold or can hold, I found that there is a much smaller number of "core" beliefs that form the root of all these variations. I use the chakras to organize them, because they are often associated with specific chakras and because it helps bring the body in.

In my work, I found that the person's developmental process correlates with the chakras when viewed from the bottom up. In other words, the earliest developmental issue of survival correlates with the base chakra (often considered the "lowest" chakra). Later developmental issues correlate with upper chakras, culminating in the crown chakra, dealing with connection with the Divine.

I will go through the chakras again, connecting them with the developmental issue that I have found most relevant in my experience of working with people over the last twenty years. Everyone is unique and individual and has his or her own patterns, but as a general guideline, this is what I found to be true.

When developmental needs are frustrated, the consequent emotions are generally fear, sadness, and anger. These emotions occur in all the chakras and when not resolved cause stagnation of the energy or hyper-energy. The only way to effectively change this pattern is to have awareness of the underlying issue and resolve it. Denial continues the pattern.

I have found it useful to use the following process of working with beliefs. Although much of this is happening on a cognitive level, it is important to be able to feel the emotions and sensations that accompany these beliefs. The more deeply these can be felt, the more effective the reprogramming will be.

When we're healing diseases, the wording (the precision of what is required) needs to be really exact. These are examples only and may not be the words that will be most healing for you. You might try these and then ask inwardly if there is something that is more specific for you. When I work with people, I may have to try a dozen different words. I am able to feel their energetic response, which tells me when we've hit the right word. This may be hard to do on yourself, which is why working with an outside person (especially someone trained) is helpful. (See page X for individual sessions.)

The base chakra deals with safety issues, being wanted, needed, and able to survive on earth. I find that many people with chronic fatigue syndrome do not have energy coming in their base chakra and are not connected with earth energy.

Negative Beliefs and Positive Healings for the Base Chakra

- Negative belief: I am not wanted.
  Healing: *I feel wanted and needed with my total passion.*
- Negative belief: I am not safe.
  Healing: *I feel safe. I am protected by Mother/Father God.*
- Negative belief: I do not want to be on this earth.
  Healing: *I feel earth is my home. I want to be here.*

The second chakra is related to trust issues and gender issues. As babies when we cry for milk and our mother responds by providing what we need, we learn to trust that we will get what we need. If the mother responds consistently and reliably in a loving fashion, we learn to feel connected, loved, and cared about. But if our mother didn't respond in this fashion, we learn that we can't trust that we will be helped.

The second chakra is also about being accepted as our gender and accepted as sensual beings. This can be learned through the other person's touch and other actions or simply picked up intuitively.

When either of these needs (for connection and reliable love and caretaking or to be accepted for our gender and sensual nature) is not met, then the negative emotions of fear, sadness, and anger take hold in this chakra, which lead to either low or excessive energy. Later, belief systems develop that go with these emotions.

Negative Beliefs and Positive Healings for the Second Chakra

- Negative belief: I am not connected with anyone.
  Healing: *I feel you are always here loving me.*
- Negative belief: I am not loved.
  Healing: *I feel loved.*
- Negative belief: No one cares about me.
  Healing: *I feel nurtured, cared for, and totally taken care of.*
- Negative belief: No one accepts me.
  Healing: *I feel accepted and approved of as I am.*
- Negative belief: I am not accepted as a (male or female).
  Healing: *I feel treasured as a* (male or female).
- Negative belief: Being sensual is bad.
  Healing: *I feel joy being sensual and sexual.*
- Negative belief: Others hurt me.
  Healing: *I feel protected and loved.*
- Negative belief: I am not "enough" (didn't get attention or bonding). I am not worthy.
  Healing: *I feel enough. I feel perfect being God's creation.*

The third chakra is about the two-year-old being supported to act, be independent, and feel important as a separate human being. Instead of being dependent on others for our needs, we are confident enough to directly get what we need for ourselves.

Negative Beliefs and Positive Healings for the Third Chakra

- Negative belief: Others don't support me.
  Healing: *I feel supported.*
- Negative belief: Others control me.
  Healing: *I feel strong and in control, aligned with God.*
- Negative belief: I am not important
  Healing: *I feel important and valued.*
- Negative belief: No one appreciates me.
  Healing: *I feel appreciated.*
- Negative belief: There is no support to be true to myself.
  Healing: *I feel supported to be true to myself. I support myself.*

The fourth chakra at the heart area is related to maturing to the point of being able to love and take care of ourselves and even extend this out to other people. It is also about being able to be mature enough to receive love from others.

Negative Beliefs and Positive Healings for the Fourth Chakra

- Negative belief: I am loved only conditionally, when I make others happy or give them what they want.
  Healing: *I feel unconditionally loved.*
- Negative belief: It's not safe to be loved.
  Healing: *I feel safe being loved by others.*
- Negative belief: It's not safe to love another.
  Healing: *I feel safe loving others intimately and unconditionally.*

The fifth chakra in the throat area is related to creativity and expression of ourselves, especially verbally. It is about feeling safe to express our ideas and emotions. It also relates to feeling that what we say is valuable. We learn to listen to others and to God.

Negative Beliefs and Positive Healings for the Fifth Chakra

- Negative belief: It is not safe to show my feelings.
  Healing: *I feel safe to express all my emotions, ideas, and truths.*
- Negative belief: No one wants to hear me.
  Healing: *I feel heard.*
- Negative belief: No one hears me.
  Healing: *I feel others love and appreciate what I have to say.*
- Negative belief: Others will criticize me if I speak my truth.
  Healing: *I feel supported when speaking my truth.*
- Negative belief: People don't want to know who I am.
  Healing: *I feel respected for who I am and what I say.*
- Negative belief: I have nothing to offer. I am not creative.
  Healing: *God creates through me. I feel all is valuable.*

The sixth chakra in the third eye is related to our visions, dreams, goals, guidance for long-term and future creativity. We learn to believe in ourselves, our yearnings, dreams, and guidance. We seek to follow our visions.

Negative Beliefs and Positive Healings for the Sixth Chakra

- Negative belief: I don't have any dreams.
  Healing: *I feel myself opening to God's dreams for me.*
- Negative belief: My dreams (heart's desires) don't come true.
  Healing: *I feel my deepest heart's desires are always supported.*
- Negative belief: I can't trust my dreams or guidance.
  Healing: *I feel my dreams and guidance are valuable. I feel God guiding my way; I feel safe following God's dreams for me.*

The seventh chakra in the crown of the head is our connection with universal energy. I see this as learning that we are all one with God; we are spiritual essences that are one with Divine Love. In this frustrated expression of this, we feel separate from God and others, whereas in the fulfilled expression we love others as ourselves.

Negative Beliefs and Positive Healings for the Seventh Chakra

- Negative belief: I am separate from God.
  Healing: *I feel Divinely Loved. I feel one with Divine Love. I feel one with God.*
- Negative belief: I am separate from others.
  Healing: *I feel related to all beings as aspects of God and myself. I feel love for all these faces of God and myself.*

Transforming Beliefs

Once we become aware of our beliefs, we have the options to choose which ones we want to keep. There are some methods out there that are believed to help with this process. One is tapping meridian lines (energy lines recognized by Chinese medicine) while affirming certain beliefs. My experience with these is that these techniques work temporarily. I have gotten more long-term changes using the hand exercise (below) and calling in the universal Divine energy to assist in the changes.

Exercise for Transforming Beliefs

1. Sense your body. Is there a place that calls to you to focus on? Is there an emotion that you feel? Where do you feel it in your body? Is there a concern or a thought? Where is it in your body?
2. Perhaps there is a belief from above that attracts you to work on. You might look through the list above and see what your mind picks out, or ask for guidance on what belief you need to work on, or imagine a meter in your mind that gives you a "meter reading" telling you how

comfortable you are with particular beliefs. You can also use muscle testing (kinesiology), pendulum, or any other method you have for getting guidance.

3. Feel where that belief resides. Tune into the physical sensations in that area. Is there a thickness or density? Is the energy flowing there? Is the energy flow fast? slow? stagnant? Does it feel heavy? How much breath can you easily bring into the area? What temperature do you notice there?

4. What emotion is in this area? (The basic emotions are anger, sadness, fear, love, and peace.) If you can't identify the emotion, try verbalizing the sensations from an I-perspective (e.g. I am heavy. I am stagnant. I feel sad).

5. Stay with the feeling and let the feeling communicate with you and tell you what happened.

6. Can you identify a core belief related to this? (Use above list.)

7. Use your non-dominant hand to represent this emotion and core belief. It might help if you visualize this as an inner child. Place this hand on your body, wherever you identified.

8. Tune in as well as you can (or use someone who is trained in this) and identify as precisely as you can what message is needed to heal this area. Keep the message as simple as possible, as though speaking with a two-year-old child.

9. Now you are going to bring in an unconditionally loving parental figure to help you. It may be God, Christ, an angel, Mary, someone in your life that has loved you, or even yourself as an adult. Check intuitively or kinesthetically which level is needed: 1) the Divine to human you, 2) the Divine working through a real human figure in your life, such as a parent, 3) your adult self to your child self. Let your dominant hand represent this love. Place it on top of the non-dominant hand.

10. As the unconditionally loving part (represented by the dominant hand), say this message out loud to the inner self (represented by the non-dominant hand). Repeat this several times. Close your eyes, and breathe this message in.

11. Have the inner self respond, by saying, *I feel* (whatever the message was). For example, if the loving part says, "I love you," the inner self responds with "I feel loved."

12. If it is difficult for you to take in this healing message, identify who is responsible for this situation. Usually our obstacles come from real-life situations we have experienced.

13. Honor what your experience is and release these feelings and beliefs by opening your eyes and expressing your feelings to an external object that you let represent whoever was externally responsible. For example, you might say to a pillow representing a parent, "You never loved me! I feel...."

14. (This step is the most important!) Now come back to the healing message and repeat the process from step 10. Be aware of how the sensations and emotions inside your body change as you take in the healing message.

15. Repeat this every day for a month. You can either do it once for a thirty-minute session or twice for fifteen-minute sessions. It will help if you link it with another routine, such as going to bed.

I often find that people will have to work on all three levels at different times, perhaps each one for a month. Similarly, they may work with a male figure for a month and a female figure another month. If you don't have a guide helping you, you might use any guidance technique (muscle testing, pendulum, asking guidance) to help you decide which you should be working with. You can also use your intuition.

Slowly, over time, with your daily commitment to the process, the positive belief gains more energy and the negative belief (which we may have been supporting our whole lives) fades away, as well as the symptoms that were there to get our attention.

You can speed up the process by trashing the negative belief and everything that bothers you about it. Then trash everything that bothers you about the positive belief. This way there is neutrality and openness to your God-self guiding you.

Themes Through Multiple Lifetimes

Sometimes we have a pattern going that continues through several lifetimes. Here is an exercise that focuses on finding the source of the themes that have been going on for lifetimes and healing this, using one, easy visualization.

- Focus on where God touches your soul and ask to find the single largest recurrent theme that has caused your biggest problems in all your lifetimes. You might see, sense, hear, or otherwise know what this is.
- Ask God to help you resolve it. See this theme surrounded by and filled with light. Receive any insights, then trash this pattern and all that bothers you about it. Release all memories and strengthen your midline, sensing God Heaven to Earth to Heaven. (Sessions and classes are helpful in doing this more completely on all levels. See back of book.)
- Thank Spirit for helping you and affirm the healed reality.

For example, my theme seed was being killed as a leader. I asked God to clear the trauma out of all my lives and to clear this fear of dying because of my following God and being a leader. I trashed all these past lives and memories. Then I asked all the good to be brought from past lives to this life for me to use.

Generational Healing

You may notice that some of your symptoms are symptoms that your parents or grandparents also had. I had a client with chronic fatigue who was nearing fifty. Both her mother and grandmother had died at fifty from chronic fatigue. We discovered a core belief that women aren't appreciated or considered worthwhile in her family. When she realized this as a generational belief, she resolved her chronic fatigue. We also trashed, then, a genetic expectation of dying at fifty years old.

The good news is that with commitment we can heal ourselves, our relatives, and help all our relations. I love how in sweat lodges we pray that all the healing in the lodge goes to all our relations. Indeed, because we are spirits in essence and one in essence, each of our individual healings heals all. So when it seems like there is just too much healing to be done on yourself, dedicate your healing also to all of your relations.

- Think of your grandparents and parents and any physical, mental, emotional, and spiritual ailments that they had. See the cause of their imbalance.

  For example, my grandfather was bald. He was overly mental. He also had many heart attacks. His lesson was to learn to be more heart-centered.
- See how it has influenced your body and if there is a similar lesson for you also. My hair falls out when I am stressed and think too much. I am focusing on being heart-centered. When you learn your lesson, the symptom doesn't need to manifest any longer.

- Put yourself and your grandparent or parent in the sun-light or under a waterfall to cleanse the imbalance. In healing our parents, we heal what we also inherited.
- Practice this with three physical ailments or more. You can do this also on emotional, mental, or spiritual levels anytime as homework.

Forgiveness and Letting Go of the Judge

Now that you've seen how much your parents and grandparents have influenced you in negative ways, it is time for forgiveness and letting go of judgments. As I looked at my own health symptoms, I was shocked to realize that they all were a carryover of some kind from a previous generation. My first response was to want to disown my parents and grandparents (and my symptoms), but this doesn't work. What we want is to forgive how our parents influenced us in negative ways, physically, mentally, emotionally, and spiritually. We want to forgive ourselves for taking these negative influences in.

On one level forgiveness is to forgive the other for their particular act of harming us. On another level it is to forgive the other for creating the impact that they did. A third level is to forgive ourselves for taking that on and creating negative beliefs and emotions around it. A fourth level is to forgive the situation and, if need be, God.

There are so many ways to forgive. If our hearts are not open, then forgiveness is the key to reopening them. Whenever my expectations aren't fulfilled, there is something to forgive. If I feel sad, angry, afraid about anything, I need to forgive myself, the other, the belief, the situation, and God, until my heart is full of love again. This may sound extreme, but forgiveness alone is able to heal physical conditions. I had one client who had forgiven her mother, and herself, but not the beliefs, emotions, and situation. That was the key needed to heal her symptom.

We forgive so that our energy can flow freely. Health is free-flowing communication. When we forgive, we are no longer identifying with our ego self, but have embraced the Miraculous, our Self, a vast freedom, allowing the energy of love to flow again.

Judgments are another way we stop free flowing communication. Whenever we judge someone else, we are judging something we are afraid of in ourselves, on some large or minute level. This negative energy restricts our overall energy and closes our hearts as well as our minds. We judge ourselves and judge others according to some kind of ideal standard, which of course can't be lived up to.

Like most egos, I used to judge a lot. I quit judging after I asked the Entity at the Casa to have God show me God's way of thinking. For three months I never judged. I allowed God to take over my mind; I was surprised by the constant flow of loving thoughts. To see the contrast value, my mind was then turned over to my thoughts. What a difference! Now I pray for God to use my thoughts daily. Every now and then I slip, but it is such a delight to leave the judging mind that there is a lot of motivation.

- Ask God to change your negative judgments into blessings instead. There is a lot more positive energy for yourself and the other in a blessing for yourself and the other.
- Give yourself a stretch by blessing our politicians and world leaders with love and ask God to guide them.

Do you think God even creates opportunities for us to learn the art of forgiving, letting go of judgments, and opening our hearts? I do, because one morning I said, "Thy Will is my will; God, use me and all that is in my life for the highest love and joy. What do you want me to learn and do today?" I was surprised by the answer. "Stay connected with Divine Love all day today. Whoever upsets you, I want you to bless them with love. Love them as Christ."

The first opportunity for me to lose my connection with Divine Love was with my husband who announced our nine-month-old building project had just died and to forget it . The second opportunity was with the builder who hung up on my husband and told him never to call again, all relationships were severed ... end of any and all conversations. We stood to lose one to three hundred thousand dollars and nine months of time and work with no explanation whatsoever nor anyway to find out. The third opportunity was with an engineer who slammed down the phone while I was talking with him. I could hardly believe it. God was being all these people blessing me with "rude acting out" so I could follow my guidance. Just two weeks before this, the Entity had shocked me by (externally) "acting out," making funny faces and saying ridiculous things that seemed insulting to me at the Casa, while internally saying, "Which are you going to trust, the external show or the internal love?" I was confused and reacted by closing my heart. I had no idea how he was serving me by giving me practice forgiving and loving him in spite of how he acted. My practice continued as I kept catching my negative judgments and emotions.

Every time I went to curse, blame, judge, or revenge these people, I remembered my guidance to forgive and love them as Christ instead. I took my guidance to heart and stretched. This lesson continued for the whole week. I was doubly challenged and tempted by my husband who reacted with all his emotions, judgments, and even got sick over the situation. I wouldn't have directly asked for this experience, just like I wouldn't have asked to practice dying for three years, but the result was liberating. I felt free from my mental negativity and emotionally reacting to external circumstances. I was amazed. My internal connection with Divine Love dominated. When I needed help loving and forgiving, I opened Joel Osteen's book, *Your Best Life Now*, and Marianne Williamson's book, *A Return to Love*.

A week later the next challenging guidance was starting the building project over and staying focused on positive thoughts. It would have been easy to Edge God Out, as Wayne Dyer says. But my Divine husband played this part of being judgmental, negative, and pessimistic, so I could become stronger at being centered in love, avoiding my pattern of reacting to his reactions. Everyone became God's face for me to learn how to love by going deeper into myself.

Before meeting John of God I would have enjoyed seeing all these people "acting rudely" as my enemies and hating them for a while. But this time, given my guidance, I couldn't have this luxury. Obviously, this entire situation was set up by God, before it even happened, for me to learn love, forgiveness, and letting go of judgments. In fact, I now remember asking the Entity to help me live Christ love and consciousness and he said, "God will help you." By God, God was helping me, but not how I expected (being given these great opportunities of loss). When I feel sorry for myself, I remember the story of Job and feel fortunate (Job lost all his possessions, family, and health having his faith tested, and then was blessed with more than before).

I know from my life that everything that happens to us is for our highest purpose, learning to be the infinite love that we are. I realize from this experience with the building and with the Entity, that God "acts out" even as rude people in our lives to strengthen our ability to love, to discipline our thoughts to be positive, and to forgive. Regardless of what treasures God strengthens us with, I know that God loves us infinitely, more than all the love we know how to express in return.

12

A Vision of Perfect Health

In the infinity of life where I am, All is perfect, whole and complete. I no longer choose to believe in old limitations and lacks. I now choose to begin to see myself as the Universe sees me, Perfect, whole and complete. The truth of my Being is that I was created Perfect, whole and complete....

You Can Heal Your Life, Louise L. Hay

Do you want perfect health?
Are you willing to focus on perfect health?

What we focus on, we create. The difficulty in being sick is that it is easy to focus on our pain, symptoms, losses, and the disease. However, it is essential to put our passion into focusing on feeling whole and healthy and living it. When we become aware that our thoughts are creating our reality and life is mirroring our thoughts, the healing begins. We become physically healed when we are able to hold the image of perfect health in our mind regardless of what the body is doing.

It is said that Christ healed people because he knew that the person's essence and blueprint was health and that disease was an illusion. He saw people as healthy. He would ask people, Are you whole? As ye believe, so shall ye be. When the person answered "yes," they were whole, they were healed. They embraced the Miraculous and attained health.

Embracing Optimal Health

A key to achieving optimal health is to be able to visualize yourself having it. It is important to be sure that your subconscious self is aligned with your conscious self with visualizing. To do this you must test yourself, or have a practitioner test to see if you are strong for your optimal health or weak. I mention this because I visualized my teeth every day being strong and healthy—and manifested more cavities. Much to my surprise, my focused attention was magnifying my fear of my teeth getting more cavities, hidden in my subconscious. I thought I had cleared this, but had not. So to work the miracle you want with visualization, clear underlying fears first, and have someone professional double-check this alignment (see back of book).

Visualization

- Twice a day, find a time and a place where you can relax and take fifteen minutes to half an hour devoted to your healing. I suggest you find a place in the sunlight (although protected from UV rays). The sun has tremendous nourishing, healing energy.
- Imagine that you are in your favorite place doing this, such as by a waterfall or lake or on a mountain top.
- Sense and visualize yourself as invigorated, energetic, strong, athletic, whole, and in perfect health.
- Support this by feeling how excited you are about being healed. Bring in feelings of happiness, peace, love, and joy. These emotions need to be strong enough to counter the daily emotions of fear, sadness, anger, and whatever other negative emotions you experience in living life.
- Give your body appreciation for being well.

- Throughout the day, act as if you are healed. It is important for the body to hold to the impression of wholeness rather than the imbalance.

For years, twice a day, I visualized myself on top of a 21,000-foot peak, feeling happy, strong, one with Spirit, and full of love for myself, my life, for others, and for the earth. I imagined hugging friends, seeing as far as the eye could reach, and feeling elated at being there.

When I started this visualization, I couldn't even walk. This did not matter to me. I knew that embracing the Miraculous would create this reality. Every step was success to me. Each day I forced myself to add a step, even though I had essentially no muscles left and couldn't walk. Adding one step every day added up to a 21,000-foot peak six years later.

Every step in this book adds up to attaining optimal health on all levels. The mind, emotions and subconscious create our physical reality. You can choose to put your faith in your blueprint of wholeness that you hold in your heart as the truth rather than the symptoms and the picture of ill-health that seem to be the reality.

I knew of a woman who was healing nicely according to her body on the BodyScan but then got literally scared to death from doctor reports. Other authors (e.g. Herbert Benson, M.D. in *Timeless Healing: The Power and Biology of Belief*) have documented examples of the power of belief to heal and to kill.

If I had let the doctors tell me what to believe, I would be dead right now. My biggest stressor on the BodyScan (an energy test of 10,000 stressors) turned out to be radiation. Doctors do their best, everyone does their best, but the truth is inside of us as our Higher Selves or God speaking with us. We have to learn to trust God within us and discipline our minds to stay true to our guidance.

An example of my being influenced early on by outside parameters rather than my inner vision was that whenever a doctor told me how sick I was, I would take that as the truth. I would spend months getting myself back on my feet, walking the few steps to the bathroom. After reading the results of my blood test, I would be back in bed unable to walk for the next week. In time, I realized that the blood tests were information that I could use as a monitor but not take as my truth. After months of practicing, I was able to maintain my mantra that *I am healing in every way, every day.* I stopped getting sick after reading the test results.

By the time the last doctor gave me only three weeks to live, I had become so centered within myself and embraced Spirit's guidance about my healing so completely, there wasn't even an iota of fear about dying. This took me three years to achieve by watching myself react and learning to trust Spirit instead.

This was one of the most important moments of my healing. My lack of trusting Spirit was the deepest source of my disease, and trusting was the deepest source of my healing. The spiritual level is the deepest source of all our imbalances. This is why embracing the Miraculous is the key to all healing; it is embracing the Divine Love that we are within us and aligning with it all around us.

When we are sick, we sometimes feel betrayed by our bodies, feel out of control, and are afraid that we won't heal. We don't expect healing to be as easy as ordering from a menu. I know that when we do expect the healing to happen, the result does manifest much faster.

Practice

- Imagine yourself totally healed.
- Drain all your fears that you won't heal to the center of the earth.

- See the Universe/God/Christ (or whoever you turn to for help) light up and bless your healthy body.
- Put this image of a healthy body in a Frisbee and send it out to collect your dream. Expect it to boomerang back to you with your wish.

You can use this exercise to manifest anything that your Self (aligned with Spirit) wills you to manifest. God doesn't manifest ego desires because they are not love and not ultimately real. So first become meditative, align with the Divine Love flowing through you, feel the love and joy in your heart, and say, "Thy Will is my Will. What is the question and answer?" Then use this exercise to manifest the answer, knowing that it will benefit all.

Lessons from the Healed Self

This is a simple, but very important transformative exercise. Step three is what differentiates it from similar processes. It is step three that changed my life and started the deepest healing processes, embracing the Miraculous.

- See where you are currently at, in terms of whatever health challenge or problem you want to focus on. (This can be on any of the four levels.)
- Visualize your ideal healed self.
- Ask this healed self what was the lesson it learned that brought it to that place (from the current state). Receive a visual, verbal, intuitive answer. If you need more help, ask God by any name to help you receive an answer. Feel your heart; ask for a symbol to symbolize the answer. Do whatever you need to do to receive an answer. This answer is your key!

Looking Through the Eyes of God

As I implied in Chapter 1, from my ego's view, I was unsuccessful. I had not been a CEO making $200,000 dollars a year like my father and brother. I didn't feel wanted or loved, didn't feel as though I was "enough," and 1001 other treasures of negative beliefs. I bet though I had the trophy for knowing every negative belief in the *Power of Negative Beliefs Book* (a book I have contemplated but not yet written). *Terror* was my subconscious name. That's what made me a good psychotherapist—I could empathize with everything a client ever thought or felt.

One of my favorite exercises to help a person drop these negative self-images is to imagine seeing yourself from the eyes of God.

When I experienced this at the Casa, I cried, feeling so in love with myself for three hours, while also listening to the music there. God did not look at my possessions, my career advancements, my earnings, or all the things that I felt "not enough" about. From the eyes of God, I was a child of God, made of the same stuff. It was as though God was the ocean, and I was the wave. We are one and the same essence. I am a manifestation of God.

As I viewed myself from the eyes of God, my focus was on all the loving intentions and actions I had lived during my life. I saw times of caring, helping, teaching, creating, adventuring, laughing, enjoying, learning, trusting, daring, forgiving, and being grateful. To God, what was most precious was my focus on developing spiritual qualities. To my utter surprise, I realized that God loved me totally.

All of my judgments about myself being "not enough" came from the opinions of others, my projections of what others thought, or from my comparing myself to others. Yet when I looked through the eyes of God, I was "enough."

What love, relief, and gratitude I felt! I not only felt "enough," I felt holy, loved by God. The things I had "failed" at were simply a part of cultural conditioning that had nothing to do with God's focus. Suddenly, I felt deeply successful.

After this, I felt empowered to see both myself and others from the eyes of God. I saw us all as Divine Love manifesting on earth. I felt more empowered to say, "Thy Will is my will" and to go inside for all my decisions. My concerns and judgments about looking a certain way or being perceived a certain way slowly faded, and I became more relaxed. When I saw judgments about myself come into my mind, I would ask guidance for help and realign with Spirit.

I focused on guidance and the visions that I felt the universe had given me to fulfill. I compared myself to myself. I asked and saw how things were happening to expand my ability to love. I felt more vulnerable than ever and yet more trusting. My façade of strength and the lack of trust underneath it was fizzling away. The truth of who I am, a being of love inspired to love, is expanding. This is an example of embracing the Miraculous.

Exploration: Seeing Yourself Through God's Eyes

- Put yourself in a relaxed state (refer to p. X).
- Drop into a theta state by sensing yourself as either 65 feet above your present location or 65 feet into the earth. (Going down is often experienced as more grounding.)
- Become one with the light and infinite space and unconditional love.
- From the perspective (of being Spirit), now look at yourself. What do you see?
- If you notice negative judgments, you are not yet in a Divine perspective. God does not have judgments! See if you can get deeper into a space of infinite love looking at your life. Embrace the Miraculous looking at yourself as Miraculous. Now who are you?

What often happens when you see yourself from the eyes of God is that you see spiritual truths about yourself, such as how loving you are, how forgiving, how grateful, and how honest and creative.

The Power of Positive Energy

It is important to put positive energy into everything that you do. Pray with love and gratitude over your body, your life, your food, your water, even your pills. My clients who have allergic reactions to something in their medications put sunlight around their pills and pray that only positive healing comes to them. This changes the vibration of anything that is negative into a positive vibration.

Masaru Emoto, a contemporary Japanese scientist, in his book, *The Hidden Messages in Water*, has beautiful photographs of frozen water crystals. The crystals have been exposed to different thoughts and feelings, even different words. The differences in water crystal shapes are dramatic evidence of the power of our attitudes. The crystals that were most beautiful were those subject to prayers of love and gratitude.

We heal our mental/emotional mindsets when we are able to focus on what brings us love and joy. We see that positive attitudes create the results that we want, and we deliberately choose not to dwell on our negative thoughts. Ask Spirit to help you to replace negative judgments with blessings for yourself and others. Remember, judgments on others are judgments about ourselves and only take away energy.

It is important to meditate and connect with the Miraculous and align with the universal energy of Divine Love. I suggest everyone meditate several times a day to heal physically and attain optimal health.

13

Healing with Spirit

Only love can … compel man to come to his highest self. And only the love experience with God can do this…. Man is, therefore, destined one day to meet this love full force. And God has willed it so. He has but one will when it comes to love, and that is to love until all have returned to Him! (p.181).
— *To Master Self Is to Master Life*, Saint Germain

Do you want the most effective efficient way to heal and grow?

When we are happy, feel loved and loving, peaceful, in bliss, these are moments when we are aligned with our Miraculous Self, with Spirit. When we are afraid, sad, and angry, we are in our ego-self, which is separate from Spirit. These emotions kick in as a reaction to our beliefs, such as thinking we are alone, not loved, not wanted, not safe, not heard, not valued, or our negative beliefs kick in our negative emotions, and so on. Many types of psychotherapy help people become aware of the beliefs that are shaping their experience and help them choose more loving beliefs. Therapy also helps empower clients to live these new beliefs.

I had been working on about six core beliefs for the past twenty years using psychotherapy. Being a psychotherapist, I was convinced this was the best way—until I found myself face-to-face with dying. I opened to being shown a deeper and faster way of aligning with Divine Love (which I have shared above in the chapter on core beliefs). There is nothing as effective and efficient as aligning with universal Divine Love for emotional healing.

The Divine at Work

One of the most amazing life-altering experiences I ever had was feeling Christ's love. Every morning at the Casa I would write God a question. Today's question was, "How do I follow Christ?

The same morning, I volunteered for physical surgery with John of God as the Entity. I was led to the back stage and told to think about God. At this point I didn't know God; I was lucky if I didn't vomit hearing the word. I had positive experiences witnessing Christ performing psychic surgeries, so I thought about Christ instead.

At Vianna Stibal's Nature Path (vianna@srv.net), where I learned to be a medical intuitive and witness Christ performing psychic surgery, they played Enya's music every day. Just at this moment at the Casa, they started playing Enya! (It was the only time I ever heard them play it.) My heart felt love like I had never felt before. I started sobbing. I knew this was Christ's love. It was the most powerful love I had ever felt. I felt loved more deeply than I knew possible.

To my surprise, something else happened. Now I was feeling love *for* Christ as though I were a disciple who had devoted my entire life to Christ. My mind watched as I committed my heart and life to Christ. Oh my God, what was happening to me? Forget the surgery; this was more than I could integrate. Vianna had said Christ was her best friend, but I didn't understand how that could be. Now I knew.

John of God, functioning as the Entity, came up to me from behind and took my hand. I experienced him as Christ. I felt as though Christ was holding my hand, leading me through the rest of my life, as I was led through the thousand meditators. We arrived at the front stage in front of an audience.

The Entity changed in a flash into a doctor and sat me down. He took a paring knife and did eye surgery on me along with two other operations in just minutes. I was wheeled out to the recovery room. When I opened my left eye, my right eye would sting, so I had to close both eyes for a couple of days and be led around by strangers in a foreign country. I felt love and trust in people guiding and feeding me. The answer to my question of how to follow Christ was to follow Christ *blindly*. I laugh at God and Christ's sense of humor.

When I was able to see again, I went back to the Entity and watched him do another eye surgery. I was a few feet from him when he deliberately looked over at me smiling, seeming to say, "Watch this!" The patient opened both eyes after the surgery, said he had no pain, could see clearly, and walked off stage. Obviously this man didn't ask how to follow Christ! God gives you what you ask for.

The biggest transformation for me was feeling Christ love me, and feeling my love and devotion for Christ. This transformed into my feeling God's love and my love and devotion for God, which transformed into seeing God in everyone and feeling love for and from everyone.

In all my years of psychotherapy, I had never felt so safe, so loved and supported by the Universe and in love with all in the Universe. I felt that I belonged on earth, was wanted, could trust others and myself and God. The work with God was much faster and more efficient in healing negative attitudes, emotions, and behaviors. It was so truly miraculous that nothing excited me more than expressing this teaching and writing it in a book.

Exercise: Meditation for Feeling Divine Love

In this meditation, you'll want to work with a mantra. With a mantra, you say it over and over and focus your consciousness on the phrase.

- Say: I feel _____ (name for God)'s love. For example, *I feel Christ's love.* Or *I feel Mary's love.* Or *I feel Divine Love.* Or *I feel the angels' love.*
- Imagine breathing in God's love. Allow the love of the universe to pour into you. Focus on your heart.
- Alternate with a mantra noting this, such as, *I feel God's love opening my heart.* Feel your heart. Continue for fifteen or more minutes feeling loved.

The Joy of Healing

Another life-altering experience I had with Christ through the Entity was after writing out two requests and putting them into the basket: "Teach me how to have Christ use me for healing" and "Release everything that blocks my heart from feeling love."

Immediately after passing the Entity, he had five hundred of us stop meditating and open our eyes. "See the power of Christ," he said. He told a man in a wheelchair to stand. He touched his body in three places and said, "Walk." The man left his chair and walked out. It was beautiful to watch this man instantly heal with Christ.

The next time I walked up to the Entity, he took hold of my right hand and yelled at me in his deep, super-stern voice. "What are you doing here? I told you to meditate. Why are you here?"

My typical response would have been to melt ten feet into the ground. My legs would have trembled and my voice would have become nonexistent. To my astonishment, as the Entity yelled at me, I noticed that my heart was opening more. I knew he was answering my request. I looked into his eyes and traveled into his soul of pure, infinite love. There was no anger, sadness, or fear anywhere. I marveled at it. As far across this whole universe of his soul, I could not see or feel anything but pure, unconditional love. At the same time, I felt a flood of love streaming from his hand into my hand, rewiring my nervous system. What an experience! Being yelled at by authority figures earlier in my life had left such a deep wound; now I was feeling bliss, pure love, as this powerful figure was yelling at me.

I told him that I had made a guided prayer meditation and handed him a CD. The Entity smiled and said, "I'll take it and sell it at the Casa."

I sat down weeping, breathing in this uncontainable love of Christ and breathing out Divine Love to the thousands of people walking up to the Entity for healing. My heart just kept expanding with love. I felt God's love healing the entire earth by using my out-breath to send out love. I was elated, serving for the next three three-hour meditations.

That night my heart was so open and light that I couldn't stop laughing. Neither could my group of eight people who had traveled to Atlanta, Georgia with me to experience the Entity. Everything cracked us up. We felt high on bliss. The blossoms and trees were so bright and seemed to call us to sniff every one of them. At the restaurant, the waiter mixed up all our credit cards and bills, so everyone paid for everyone else's dinner.

We went outside the restaurant to get a ride. We looked at each other and couldn't contain our laughter. My husband, Carlos, asked, "What taxi will pick us up? We look like we just escaped from the mental hospital!" We were all dressed in white, several of us holding our hotel pillows because meditating on the hard seats was so painful.

So I called our hotel service. They informed me the van was not available.

"But we look like escapees from the mental hospital! And besides, we have no way to return your pillows, which we took to meditate with John of God. So unless you pick us up, we'll remain stuck here with your pillows standing outside Toys R Us."

The hotel desk lady laughed and said she would come immediately. She said she had never seen a group of such happy people in her life. We had all received such deep healings; it's true that we were indeed embracing the Miraculous.

Exercise: Meditation for Feeling Yourself as Divine Love

In this mantra meditation, we progress from feeling God's love (or Christ, the angels, or whoever you choose) to feeling ourselves as this love.

- Meditate, breathing in Divine Love and breathing out Divine Love for fifteen minutes or more.
- Use the mantra, *I am Divine Love*. Focus on breathing into your heart and feel it opening.

You Are Love

My experience of feeling, sensing, and breathing infinite, Divine Love with the Entity (coming through John of God's body) continued to deepen. I realized my life motivation was now to embrace what Christ was, to embrace this miraculous Divine Infinite Love each moment of life.

How do we become this love that Christ was showing me (via the Entity) was possible for all of us? One way is to practice the dying meditation (Chapter 4).

Christ's answer (in Glenda Green's book, *Love Without End*) was "You are Love" (p. 57). "Beingness is above doing, and the name of your beingness is Love" (p. 60).

The love I feel with Christ and these Entities of Light is phenomenal. Realizing love is who we are and that we can increase this awareness seems to be a major first step. Realizing that the natural state of all life is love can help us remember who we are.

Dogs are a great example of this. Often they are unconditionally loving. I have even experienced a dog in tremendous pain licking me with unconditional love. Nature is a great reminder of being and radiating love.

Exercise: Experiencing Yourself as Love(d)

Here are several methods that may help support your experience of yourself as love and as being loved.

1. Find a flower, such as a bright yellow sunflower. It will help you become one with the flower if you can, in the first person, present tense, describe yourself as the flower. Example: *I am yellow. I am radiant. I am shining love in every direction. I am beautiful. I am love, whether anyone sees me or not. I am joy. I am optimism. I am love regardless of what is happening to me in my external environment. I am love. I am Divine Love. Divine Love is my essence.*

2. Think of times you experienced your being as love. Embrace this, magnify it, and remember it often. Look for ways to be this state of love as often as possible.

3. Look into the mirror and say, "I unconditionally love you." Repeat this until you feel unconditional love for yourself. This might take a half hour or an hour. Do this daily.

Divine Therapy

I have found that the depth of Divine Love I have experienced has changed my beliefs and behaviors. By sensing God, feeling God's love, and knowing I am one with God, my ego's wounded core beliefs are becoming non-issues. To my utter amazement, I realized that meditating and healing my relationship with God healed the source of my emotional dysfunctions.

When we focus on love and light rather than fear, the love expands. This is exactly what I feel happened to me and how we are empowered by focusing on our connection with God and on our essence as love.

During meditations at the Casa, with a hundred other people, with beautiful music and the high energy of all the Entities and angels healing everyone, I've had emotional healings that went to the source of my wounds. Abuse, hurts, the pain of a lifetime lifted when I felt God love me.

I saw the essence of my mother come to me as an unconditionally loving mother that was similar to Christ's essence. I was blown away. I was loved so deeply and with such fulfillment that forgiveness was not even necessary. All my emotions of sadness, anger, and fear were melted into feeling loved by my mother and my loving her.

The next day the same healing happened with my father. His essence came to me like Christ's. I felt saturated with love. Unconditional love at this depth replaced all prior experiences, memories, and grievances.

This experience with both parents went from an experience in meditation to my feeling loved and loving my parents when I physically visit them.

Exercise: Experiencing Your Parents Transformed

This is an opportunity to clear unresolved feelings with a parent and have your parent (figure) respond in a way they never did—a way that is healing and helps transform your relationship with that parent and your core beliefs about yourself. Note: If the first part of working with the pillows in Gestalt-fashion is too difficult, you may skip to the step of writing a letter instead.

- Set up four pillows, one to represent your God-self, one your self now, one your inner child, and one a parental figure (whomever feels most appropriate to work with).
- Begin sitting on the pillow that represents the God-self. Feel your unconditional love and your wisdom and ability to see the whole situation clearly. From this perspective, assess what is needed.
- Move to the self pillow (as your current age) and hold your inner child (pillow) so that it feels safe. Allow the inner child to speak or, if preferred, for the adult to communicate the child's feelings to whichever parent is most important in the moment. Put that parent's representative (pillow) in front of you. Make sure you speak in the present tense, as though the child's feelings or grievances are current right now. Close your eyes and go inside, sense your body and any tight or aching areas, feel any emotions. Begin by expressing those emotions, such as "I feel angry," or "I feel sad." Say whatever you need to in order to express yourself fully. You can say anything you want or do anything you want to this pillow, knowing you are safe and the pillow can't hurt you.
- To deepen the experience, write a letter to this parent reinforcing what you've just said, expressing anything you haven't fully gotten out. Allow yourself to be as adamant as you want. You can go back and forth between the let-

ter-writing and the pillow talk, if you want. End this letter forgiving your parent, your beliefs, the circumstance,
and yourself.

- Burn the letter. Notice how it burns. If it doesn't totally
burn, you need to write an additional letter. If it goes up
in a poof, you're complete thus far.
- Do whatever seems appropriate to let go and symboli-
cally transform this relationship with the original parent.
- Ask God (by whatever name) to infuse your image of
this parent with unconditional love. I suggest you either
take the original parent pillow and cover it with a cloth
or something that changes the character of it for you or
get a new pillow to represent this transformed parent.
- See this parent as God loving you.
- Now sit in the parent pillow and feel yourself as this
God-infused parent, talking to the pillow that represents
the child. Respond to everything that the child expressed
concern about in the above steps. Use present tense, I-
language, e.g. "I love you. I'm sorry...."
- Return to the child pillow and respond.
- Continue this process until you feel filled with love from
this parent and love toward your parent free of any grievances.
- End by sitting in the God-pillow. How is the situation
now? How has the relationship changed? Is there any
more work that needs to be done? If so, go back to the
appropriate pillow.
- After this process is complete, you might repeat it with
the other parent, or save this for another time.

Over time, be aware of how this changes your relationship with this parent and changing the story you hold about
your life. (If you enjoyed this process and want more help,
contact a Gestalt therapist, a Psychosynthesis therapist, or

myself.) You are embracing the Miraculous, changing your perception within, and noticing the external mirroring.

The Course of Miracles calls miracles a change in perception. I consider what happened to me to be a miracle that I'd like everyone to easily experience. The most wonderful part is that I know that the Divine Love is the doer and the miracle will just as easily happen for you as it did for me by focusing on Divine Love.

When we feel separate from Spirit, it takes a lot of effort to change ourselves and release our fears. But when we open our perception to knowing that we are drops in the ocean of Divine Love, the momentum of the ocean's love easily embraces us and carries us with it. Allowing this ocean of love to heal us is much easier than trying to do it ourselves.

It amazes me that all my negative mental attitudes and emotions have healed more in one year embracing the Miraculous than in all the rest of my life, doing psychotherapy and being a psychotherapist.

14

The Magic Moment

*When you are in the present moment you are in God. That is the
true meaning of meditation, the true meaning of prayer, the true
meaning of love ... it is God flowing through you (p. 496).*
—*The Book: An Introduction to the Teachings of
Bhagwan Shree Rajneesh*, Osho

Would you like to live in the Magic Moment?

We develop a relationship with the Divine by setting
aside time to feel and merge with God. Most people use
meditation and prayer for this. Although I use the word
"meditation," some of what I describe is very similar to forms
of prayer such as Centering Prayer, developed by Father
Thomas Keating. In this chapter, I talk about my favorite
ways of having that inward time as well as the secret of living
in the moment, which makes that moment magical. My hope
for myself and others is to get to the point where everyday
living is embracing the Miraculous each moment as a form
of meditation and prayer.

The Power of Meditation

Everything you've learned in the book can be integrated
in the meditation process. Much has been written about how
to meditate and why it works. I think the most valuable aspect of it is that it is a tool that helps bring people into the
theta state, which allows them to be more spacious and re-

ceptive on all four levels—mental, emotional, physical, and spiritual. Meditation can be used to amplify your alignment with God. Putting in meditation time when you connect-in on this deep level allows you to change negative beliefs and emotions.

I don't know about you, but I've meditated thirty years and hated it twenty-eight of those. Often meditation was a lot of boring work (like TM repeating one mantra over and over). It also took a lot of concentration to track body sensations, thoughts, and feelings continuously (Vipassana-types). Although this had a long-term benefit for me (allowing me years later to be able to identify with anyone else's emotions, thoughts, sensations, disease, and distinguish them from mine), I don't know that these forms of meditation are generally so helpful to people if they grow to hate meditation. I have found the two forms of meditation I describe below to be much more powerful, loving, and lead to formless meditation as described at the end.

Even though I was suffering so many years in my sitting meditation practice, I intuitively knew that meditation was a key to harmonizing with God and living in the present, so I endured it. When I learned to use sitting meditation to be with God, this changed everything. I went from finding it hard to endure ten minutes of meditation to falling in love with meditating with God, even for three or five hours at the Casa without a break.

Generally, people progress from more structured meditations that help develop concentration to more formless meditations, where one simply sits in a receptive state. I will start here with mantra meditations, which are more focused, and move toward less structured practices.

It is preferable if you meditate the same time each day for the same length and meditate in the same spot. It is sort of like a signal set up to you and to your guides. I find that my guides now wake me up with a rush of cosmic energy thirty minutes to an hour before my day begins so that I never miss my meditation.

A related practice is reading inspirational literature. It is not exactly meditation, but it is close. I spend time every evening with some kind of spiritual reading and feel that it keeps me growing.

Spiritual Mantras

I've found that using this mantra meditation is the fastest and easiest method for quickly deepening with Spirit. In this mantra meditation, you pick phrases that personally speak to you in the language that you speak. I find that chanting phrases in a different language does not open me up as much as finding phrases that are personally meaningful.

I also find that intuitively allowing the phrases to change keeps me awake, deepening and expanding rather than dulling my consciousness. In my method, I allow the phrases to fade out as I totally absorb and embody this energy. There is time to pause and be that which I have been attuning to. This pause could last only a few seconds in the beginning or (later) for a very long time. The depth itself (oneness with Spirit) becomes my guide, leading me to pick up the phrase again or to take on a new phrase that continues deepening my state. In the beginning, you will change mantras more often in order to keep your attention; later, you can stay with a mantra longer. I find that when I work with a mantra, it opens me as a channel for waves of universal energy that literally light me up. You can get an idea of how to do this by listening to my mantra meditation on my webside or by ordering my DVD (see back of book). In my experience, an hour mantra meditation is so powerful it can achieve results equivalent to ten days of awareness meditation. Enjoy.

Here is the basic practice.

- Start with the mantra, "I share God's presence." As you say it, focus on sensing your body, feeling God's presence in every cell of your body, if you can.
- Repeat this fifty times (or for a few minutes) out loud until it naturally fades out and there are no thoughts for a few seconds or more. Then go back to the mantra and start again. The longer you work with the mantra, the longer this space of peace and love becomes.
- Notice feeling emotions of love, happiness, joy, peace. These aren't the only feelings you may have. Perhaps sadness, anger, or fear may come up as you work with this mantra.
- When your mind starts to think of unrelated worries or thoughts, refocus by repeating the same mantra or saying a new mantra like, "I feel God's love." If you don't feel anything after five or ten minutes, try, "I am opening my heart to feeling God's love or presence." This allows you to be more open to feeling.
- Have your intention be to deepen your spiritual connection, and notice this happen throughout the meditation.
- Doing this meditation for an hour or less, you will usually feel enormous love and peace.

Mantra Samples

There are an infinite number of mantras. You can make up your own. It is always best to keep them simple. Here are some ideas.

- I share God's presence (or I share "the presence," Christ's presence, angelic presence)
- I sense Father God's presence, heaven to earth.

- I sense Mother God's presence, earth to heaven.
- I am one with God (or Christ, Mary, the angels, the spiritual hierarchy, the universe, light, mother earth etc.)
- I am Divine Love (or Divine light, beauty, wisdom).
- I feel Divine Love.
- I breathe in Divine Love.
- I breathe in Divine Love and out Divine Love.
- I breathe in and out Divine Love that is healing all.
- I am radiant love (unconditional love).
- I am (or feel) loved by the Universe (or by God, Christ, the angels, Mary, the Creator etc.).
- I love God (or Christ, Mary, my guides, the earth, humanity).
- I am light.
- I see and feel my entire body as light.
- I am infinity.
- I see myself from the eyes of God.
- I love myself.
- I love my symptoms.
- I love my family.
- I embrace the Miraculous
- I am healing on all levels in all ways.
- I am healing_____. I feel the healing. I feel healed.
- I see myself being healed. (I see _____being healed.)
- I am healed. My _____is healed.
- I feel (or I am) optimal health. (I feel optimal health in all my cells.)
- I feel supported by_____.
- The universe is conspiring for my highest love and joy.
- I am grateful for my life (for God, for my health, for my talents, family, friends, food, air, water, home, money, job, the earth…)
- I celebrate my life.
- I am blessed. I feel blessed.
- God blesses and loves all.

- I am forgiveness.
- I forgive anyone who has offended me.
- I see light filling and blessing the earth.
- I see light filling my home, family, all people, all countries.
- I see light filling anyone who has offended me.
- I see light filling people in positions of power.
- I see all existence as blessed with light.
- I bless all I see with love and light.

Ending a Meditation Period

Meditation is a time for the body to relax. Enjoy this as much as you can. When you are ready to finish, say "I feel totally refreshed, light, and invigorated."

When you get up, stomp your feet on the ground. Feel the bottoms of your feet touching the ground. Feel your body, and breathe deeply into your pelvis.

Get a drink of water and bless it with sunlight, love, gratitude and anything else that seems appropriate. Bring yourself to this present moment by walking around looking at your surroundings and feeling your body. Does everything look brighter and more alive?

Living in the Present Moment

For thirty years, my dream was to embrace the Miraculous by living in the present moment every moment. For me, this is living with heightened aliveness, aware each moment of body sensations, emotions, thoughts, and my connection with God.

Reaching this and staying in this state is not easy. For me, it has been a process. I had tasted being present while hiking, skiing, dancing, and meditating in ashrams, but then I'd lose the Now. I read books saying that living in the Now was simple, but the "how to" was missing.

After I began my relationship with the Casa, one morning I woke up with the guidance of how to live in the present moment continuously. When we do this, life becomes quite magical. For me, everything in the natural world looks brighter and more beautiful—as if looking at diamonds filled with rainbows. My heart is grateful and appreciates everything it experiences. Each encounter with people (and animals) feels like a gift from the universe teaching me something about love. The beauty I see, the love and gratitude I feel when I am living in the present, is truly living *heaven on earth*, embracing the Miraculous.

In this state, my mind is full of wonder and awe. It is not carrying around its usual "stuff," worrying about the future or the past, or "thinking" about things—unless information or thinking is needed.

What keeps us from this incredible present moment is the constant chatter usually filling the mind. The subconscious mind's job is to protect the body, so it thinks about fears of what has happened in the past and what might happen in the future.

As we've heard so many times, thoughts create reality. The choice is whether habitual (probably subconscious) thoughts based on fear are creating your life, or conscious thoughts based on love are creating your life. When I am unaware of what is going on in my mind, habitual worrying happens, and I feel anxious, stressed, and uptight. When I choose conscious loving thoughts, my body feels loved, relaxed, spacious, happy, and present.

The journey to living now in the magic moment, dancing with God, starts with choosing which of these realities you want.

The following instructions, verses, and photographs from my book *The Magic Moment* (order at the back of this book) will stimulate you to experience the Divine presence of Now. Continued practice maintains this magical Now. It is simple, fun, and rewarding when you choose to live Now, to live love. Strive to embrace the Miraculous each moment.

Instruction for Oneness Meditation (using photographs)

The central practice of this particular form of meditation is becoming one with what you see in nature and then shutting your eyes and feeling what happens inside of you physically, emotionally, mentally, and spiritually. Going inside and noticing your experience deepens this oneness. It is a process of allowing feelings and sensations to be the feelings and sensations of the object you've become one with.

Ute Indian vision quests (as taught to me by Joseph Rael, Beautiful Painted Arrow) are done for three or more days using a similar process. It is believed that when you identify with an aspect of nature and speak as that being, you are one with it. Becoming one with the object and with yourself experiencing the object is in the state of oneness present in the Now. During vision quests, this experience of oneness allows you to receive visions of your life.

Gestalt art therapy also uses this technique of speaking as the object or person in order to know it and yourself more intimately. It is helpful if you can adopt the attitude of a young child, who has fun playing being a queen, king, bandit, dead people, or whatever the child can imagine. Think of how children become these things with their whole beings. See if you can do the same. Just do your best and know this is perfect. The more you play with it, the easier and better you'll do it. Just keep playing.

In our practice, we'll use the photograph pages that follow. Look at the photo and read the verse (all at once or line by line). Then savor each line and become one with it by shutting your eyes and noticing what happens. Notice physical sensations, thoughts, emotions, and spiritual connections.

I suggest that you spend several minutes doing this as you work with each page.

Let's begin.

- Look at the first photograph. Imagine becoming one with the mountain.
- What happens physically? Go inside by closing your eyes. Notice physical sensations.
- What do you feel emotionally? Go inside.
- What spiritual connections happen?
- Practicing all the different ways you can describe yourself as this object will help you to connect and become one with this and other objects more quickly.

Photo #1

- Use the I-am format for each quality you experience. For example, *I am the mountain peak. I am standing tall. I am rugged. I am solid. I am joining earth to heaven and heaven to earth. I am greatness. I am solid confidence.*

Now look at the second photograph and become one with the waterfall. Repeat the above process, tuning into the various levels. For the I-am part, try, *I am cascading water. I am letting go. I am falling. I am changing. I am flowing with God.*

Photo #2

Look at the third photo-
graph. Repeating the above
process, say, *I am a flower. I am
colorful. I am beautiful. I am deli-
cate. I am vulnerable. I am love.*

What happens when you
say, *I am beautiful?* Do you see
yourself as beautiful? Notice
what emotions occur and what
beliefs or self-recognitions are
present. Do you believe that
you are love and beauty? What
happens when you become one
with something beautiful in nature that seems like a clear ex-

Photo #3

pression of God? Many of us can see the beauty and divinity
in nature but not in ourselves.

All sorts of thoughts, emotions, and sensations may come
up which seem to negate the verse. You may, for example,
feel tense, angry, and excluded. That's fine. If we were perfect, then we wouldn't be on this playground earth. If you
have reactions like this, go back to Chapter 10, focusing on
emotions and review the exercise in Loving Your Symptoms.
Say, "I unconditionally love myself for feeling _____
while saying, *I am beautiful.*"

You want to try to stretch your concept of self. See yourself from the eyes of God or from your Higher Self.

There are fifty-two photo-mantra combinations that can
be viewed in *The Magic Moment* book (order at the end of this
book). I recommend working with one a week.

This exercise with the photos teaches you how to tune in
and become one. This is a tremendously powerful practice
for staying in the present as you go through your life. By

keeping aware of details in the physical world, it keeps you connected to the world around you.

By using the format, "I am (and naming the object or quality)," my awareness of myself is expanded. I am connecting the external to my internal world in the present moment. So, for example, if I see light on a flower, I feel my own flowering and my own light nature. This fascinating, always-changing experience becomes much more attractive and intriguing than the mental routines and worries about the past and future. After practicing for some time, I don't even need to verbalize the connection by saying, "I am ____." I just automatically am that. It makes for a very pleasurable experience in nature.

Just as with the mantra meditation, in which you start with repeating the mantra and eventually become one with it, so much so that you don't need the words, here you start with the practice of using the I-am phrase to deliberately merge with the object, and later don't need the phrase—until you lose the connection. So just as in sitting meditation, when you notice your mind dreaming about something, you come back to the mantra, here when you are no longer connecting with the environment, you come back to using the I-am practice.

One of my favorite practices is using the mantra, *I am in the magical now*. As I use this phrase, my eyes take in all the magic and become one with it instantly. My heart expands in gratitude. When I stop noticing the magic, I return to saying, *I am living in the Miraculous*, or *I am Now*, or *I share God's presence*, whatever gets me back into the magical moment. In this now, I join as one with the sky, the sun, light, trees, meadows, flowers, and so on. You can train yourself to enjoy relishing the now by paying attention to details. Singing songs, humming, mantra prayers like *I love God*, *I love the Miraculous*, *I love* (whatever comes into view) are variations you can use to live in the present moment.

Both the oneness meditation (with photos and objects of nature) and the sitting mantra meditation reinforce each other.

Formless Meditation

Many spiritual teachers have said that we use techniques until we don't need them anymore. I have found a progression in my own meditation to a more formless practice. I just sit and feel the light and energy streaming into my body. My meditation time is now a time of openness and receptivity, the time when I most often receive guidance. I think this is what the mystics most often experienced, a simple state of communion with the Divine.

Most of us need some warm-up time. We don't just sit down and feel communion with God right off the bat. Like all relationships, this relationship takes time to develop. I encourage you to use the mantras and oneness meditation (as well as any other forms that work for you) until they seem to drop away on their own, or you are drawn to this simple practice of presence.

15

Integrating the Four Levels to Achieve Optimal Health

Throughout my journey to the Hereafter, I saw firsthand that Love is a Divine, living energy of unparalleled might and magnificence.... Love is our state of being (p. 90). We are great, powerful, mighty spiritual beings of Light, living in a physical world with dignity, grace and purpose (p. 111).
—*The Secrets of the Light: Spiritual Strategies to Empower Your Life ... Here and in the Hereafter,* Dannion Brinkley

Do you want to live more of God's potential coming through you?

Now that we've gone through each of the four levels and practiced numerous exercises, it is time to put it all together. In this chapter, I'll tell you how I used many of these processes with a chronic problem and provide an exercise for you to look at what optimal health on these levels would look like for you and how to live this vision.

A Personal Example

I have found that most of us come into this world with some weakness that, along with bringing pain, will become a vehicle for growth, learning to love, and forgive and guides us to our life treasures. This is the case with my mouth and neck area.

The Grave's disease leeched the calcium from my teeth and caused tooth decay and gum loss. Radiation and heavy metals were both great dangers to me, and I had to have all my mercury fillings replaced as well as my metal-backed bridge. Needless to say, there was much healing to do on my teeth.

I will take you through my process below. Using all the methods I've shared in this book brings about instant healing. It is important to understand that each symptom has many contributing factors, and it takes tremendous persistence and commitment to heal all the various aspects. Just as one aspect improves, another will call for more improvement also. This may seem like a backward step, but not necessarily. It is like tuning a symphony. The more everything is tuned up, the more you notice any aspect that is not in tune. It is a continual process of refinement.

In this description, you'll see how I used the various exercises in this book to address all of the levels of healing. I used Yuen Method to open up my receptivity to Universal Energy by putting in the sun as my trash everything that bothered me about all my teeth falling out. I also trashed memories and all that bothered me about knocking out other people's teeth from a past life in Mexico.

You will recognize healing on the emotional level that relates to the inner child in dialogue with God, the inner child in dialogue with the adult self, and the inner child in dialogue with transformed parental figures. On the mental level, there was affirming new beliefs, visualizing health, and dialoguing with the healed self; on the spiritual level, there was dialoguing with God and taking on a God perspective; and the physical level involved changes in the physical care of my teeth.

Doing the Healed Self exercise helped me get out of my denial about my symptom and gave me the inspiration that there was a higher purpose to my ailment. This energized me to get into the nitty-gritty details needed to get well. I visualized myself with healed teeth and gums and asked them what had been learned to succeed in getting there. The lesson was the teeth feeling totally radiant with God's love, so much so that there was the energy to re-grow these structures.

Often you'll find that a symptom in the body holds the same energies, impressions, and feelings as the wounded inner child. If you can allow yourself to speak from the symptom, you will recognize this voice. So for example, when I listened to my weak teeth, I found them sounding just like me as a young child, hiding under the chair, pretending to be a cat. The child (and teeth) felt unwanted, unloved, not cared for. My teeth felt helpless, attacked, angry, and sad, because as a child my parents had forced me to have four teeth pulled so that I could have braces. This belief of being victimized carried through my life up to this time. I had several accidents with my teeth knocked out, as well as loosing teeth with my Grave's disease and through cavities. The bacteria causing the cavities was a metaphor of my parents taking out my teeth.

I needed to start with feeling loved by God because I had experienced so much personal trauma with my parents. I had not felt loved, and needed to start with love, so I turned to God. Unlike with my parents, I felt God wanted me, and I felt God's love, support, and care for me. I felt this first as a whole, then in the chakras, and later zeroed in on my weakest area, my teeth, sending this same love into my teeth.

This took the form of giving and receiving that was described in the process of reprogramming core beliefs. I took time with this process. I might work for a month with God (as Mother, then God the Father), saying "I love you," and the teeth taking that in, affirming, "I feel loved." Then

I would work with God saying "I support you" or "I want you" and the teeth receiving this, saying, "I feel supported," "I feel wanted."

After working with God, I was able to imagine God coming through my parents in the form I described at the end of Chapter 13 (Experiencing Your Parents Transformed). Through this, my child was able to express her feelings first to the original parent; then I spoke to the transformed (God-infused) parent (Mother and then Father) and gained an understanding of how loved I was and how their actions were not to hurt me but rather to make me more beautiful. Having my teeth pulled was an expression of my parents' caring for me. Understanding this, I saw how my belief of being attacked led to losing many teeth, and that this belief was false. Now I could join with them in embracing that decision to pull my teeth and see it as loving. At last, I felt totally supported.

After this process, I felt empowered, loved, and supported. Just as my inner child was now healed, my teeth could be healed and could grow strong. I then went on to the forgiveness exercise. I forgave myself for having all of my feelings that I and my teeth were not wanted, loved, cared for, or supported. I forgave myself for having these beliefs that caused me to feel attacked and lose my teeth, have cavities and gum disease. I forgave my parents for pulling out my teeth. I forgave all the people who knocked out my teeth and all the dentists that gave me pain. Forgiveness is needed on so many levels; we have to forgive events, conditions, beliefs, emotions. We forgive not for other people but to align with our Self.

Next, I went back and talked with my inner self and my teeth as the adult. I apologized for my denial and avoidance and for my lack of care and love. I forgave my teeth for all the pain I had felt. I loved my teeth and every emotion that I held about them. (See Loving Your Symptoms in Chapter

10.) With chronic conditions, there can be many layers of emotions. It's important to have the attitude that you'll never give up on yourself. This is like taking on God's attitude.

Finally I was able to accept my teeth as they were with their needs. I had been in denial, hoping they were stronger than they were. My teeth wanted brushing three times a day, pick, floss, proxibrush, irrigator, minerals, calcium, herbs, homeopathy, and lots of love.

I also practiced working from a God-perspective. (For exercise, review *Seeing Yourself Through God's Eyes* in chapter 12.) It was only from God's perspective that I could look at my situation and see that my teeth were serving me by stretching me to unconditionally love one of the most difficult situations of pain in my life and to love some of the most difficult people in my life. I had to learn forgiveness.

I also saw that from God's view, my essence is an evolving spirit that is becoming aware of being one with God and unconditionally loving all. My teeth are certainly not the eternal part of my being, but are a device designed by God for my growth. From this perspective, I could better love my teeth and forgive myself for holding the illusion that the body is most important.

Having God's view is very important, because lacking this, I had viewed my teeth as an enemy because they brought so much pain. To endure the pain, I often tried denial and avoidance. Yet in my experience, healing is communicating within and between all levels. Optimal health is a free flow of communication.

In this book I have given detailed experiences for you to heal physically, mentally, emotionally and physically. When you have integrated this wealth of healing, there are shortcuts. God may use us to create miraculous results instantly on all levels within minutes. Optimal health may be lived this moment on all levels.

Living Optimal Health

Optimal health is multi-faceted. You can look at optimal health on all four levels.

Spiritual Optimal Health is:

- Being aware of feeling Divinely Loved.
- Unconditionally loving God by all names with all your heart, soul and mind.
- Unconditionally loving yourself.
- Unconditionally loving others.
- Forgiving yourself, your attitudes, emotions, others, God, circumstances.
- Being nonjudgmental.
- Living the Magic Moment.
- Living your Higher Purpose and Thy Will serving God and humanity.

Mental Optimal Health is:

- Transforming negative beliefs of fear into love.
- Living positive beliefs.
- Choosing to live enlightenment, Christ Consciousness now.

Emotional Optimal Health is:

- Living love, joy, happiness, laughter, peace....
- Choosing to transform fear, anger, sadness into love.
- Living a balanced life having loving relationships, career, higher purpose, home, play, recreation, rest, money.

Physical Optimal Health is:

- Loving, appreciating and accepting your physical body, others, and your surroundings.
- Having plenty of energy to create your Higher Purpose.

- Having a lack of symptoms or being at peace with them.
- Nurturing yourself with water, good food, exercise, water.

I see the spiritual level as the foundation for the other three. If any one of the four levels is neglected, it will pull down all the areas. So it is important that we love ourselves by focusing on all the areas. From 1 to 100%, rate each area of your life. You want a balance between all four areas. If one is low, concentrate on this one to equalize it with the others.

At the beginning of the book, there is an exercise in which you imagined how your life would be if you constantly felt a connection with Divine Love. I passionately wanted to live my imagination of Divine Love every moment, so I asked John of God as the Entity to "help me live Christ love and consciousness." I secretly thought it would take a lifetime or more to embrace this reality though. Do any of you have this secret excuse? My spirit guides knew my soul desire for "enlightenment" was now, the only moment that exists, and didn't buy into my secret. They guided me to Blockbuster's video store where I found Neale Donald Walsch's movie, *Conversations with God*. Immediately I read his *Conversations With God: Books 1, 2, and 3* plus more. But the burning phrase that changed my expectation of taking a lifetime to fully Embrace the Miraculous totally, all the time, now was:

"If you want your life to take off, then change your idea about it. About you. Think, speak, and act as the *God* you are." ... "It will entail constant moment-to-moment monitoring of your every thought, word, and deed. It will involve continued choice-making constantly. This whole process is a massive move to consciousness" (Neale Donald Walsch, *Conversations with God*, pp. 76, 77).

God spoke to me via Neale. To me the message was— there is no waiting ... be ... embrace the God-self that you are now. My secret was really about laziness thinking—that tomorrow I'd wake up. God again was done waiting, but I didn't need dying or pain to motivate me. Joy and love is plenty to motivate me now and I hope that's all you need. I urge you to do the following homework and not put it off for another moment or day or lifetime. Now is a great moment to envision your Optimal Life on all four levels..

Life Homework: Embracing the Miraculous and Attaining Optimal Life

- Take a piece of paper and write down the **mental beliefs** that you would cherish and like to be living by. You might use colored pencils or other art materials. Have fun with this and hang it somewhere you can see it. You might review the core beliefs chapter and see if you have incorporated some of the positive beliefs associated with the various chakras.
- Commit to transforming fears into love.
- What would your **ideal emotional** life be like? Imagine that there is no limit to the joy and happiness possible for you. Imagine that God (by whatever name) is giving you permission to have the most joyous life possible. Can you imagine feeling divinely loved and being in joy and peace regardless of external circumstances?
- Imagine what **optimal physical health** would look like for you.
  - What can you do to achieve and maintain this? (e.g. physical check-ups, bioenergetic check-ups, diet, exercise, water, sleep, friends, lifestyle, etc.)
- Now that you have experienced sensing God's energy, feeling God's love, hearing, seeing, and knowing God, how would you imagine your ideal life having this **spiritual** connection be even deeper? Commit to sensing and feeling this connection each day.

- Look for objects that represent this connection (or make them) and place them in view. Do you have a teacher who inspires you?
- Identify other ways for supporting this connection (e.g. commitment to meditation time, prayer, reading spiritual literature, special places, nature, music, singing, hiking, dancing, skiing, or other activities).
- Strive to follow *Thy Will* 100%.
- Strive to live in unconditional love for God, yourself, and others.
- Strive to forgive and not to judge God, yourself, or others.
- Strive to live in the magic of the present moment.

Surprise Blessings: Being Embraced

I was elated when I walked out of baggage claim and saw my taxi driver standing next to John of God who had open arms waiting to greet me. I dropped my bags and ran to give him a hug and kiss with all the love and gratitude I had wanted to express to him for the last eighteen months. This embrace with John of God was one of the most healing embraces of my life. His serving God had helped me find and serve God.

I was so grateful to him. A million thanks could not have expressed the depth of my gratitude. His taxi arrived, and he turned and embraced me a second time. I felt in this second embrace that he had received my gratitude completely and that he knew I was carrying this book and was giving me a blessing for all the work I had done.

The next day at the Casa I went up to the Entity who blessed the book and endorsed it. I felt totally embraced by the Christ-love coming through the Entity. In the last eighteen months, it felt like I had received endless love and experienced ongoing miracles as I devoted my life to God, living *Thy Will*.

When I returned home to Colorado I received word that Blue Dolphin Publishing had accepted the manuscript. This had been the only publisher I approached. I had felt guided to this publisher after finding a blue dolphin made of glass stuffed absentmindedly in a bookshelf by my husband six months previously. God found the perfect fit for me with this publisher.

I had been triply embraced—by John of God, by the Divine Love coming through the Entity, and by finding the perfect publisher for this book.

Blessings to You

May you have the courage to align with and follow Divine Will.
May you be blessed by and open to receiving the Miraculous, Divine Love, God by all names each moment.
May you live the Miraculous, being the Divine Love that you are and attaining optimal health on all levels.

Do you feel that you need more inspiration? I want you to know all is possible with Spirit. Remember, I went from 95% dead, unable to walk, seriously depressed, and not knowing God, to optimal physical health, a joyful outlook, embracing the Miraculous, living in love and in the present moment.

I know that you can have your heart's dreams, because your dreams were created by the Miraculous long ago. Visions have led my life, visions that my mind thought were impossible. My willingness to say yes and follow guidance one step at a time taught me how to embrace the Miraculous. Say yes to feeling embraced by the Miraculous (and don't forget to embrace yourself and others as well).

Perhaps you feel the universe has opened you to the infinite creativity of God bursting forth. Then while you're embracing the Miraculous, remember what my editor Paul Clemens says, "For God's sake, relax!" and treat yourself as the precious treasure of love that you are. "Love, care, and respect yourself as you would do for the Dalai Lama, Thich Nhat Hanh, or anyone else you respect so the busyness doesn't possess you" (paraphrased p. 27), as the author, speaker Joan Borysenko suggests in her book, *Inner Peace for Busy People*. Have you ever seen a tree tense, or in a hurry?

Embracing the Miraculous is trusting that God's joy and passion is moving us in perfect timing with the resources and space for God's will to happen.

The Divine Love connection within ourselves Embracing the Miraculous in the present moment is God's ultimate goal for us. Our external goals and challenges are merely excuses to practice living Divine Love, living being the Miraculous one with God. There is only one presence, that is God. There is only one time, now. There is only one goal, to wake up to our being the Miraculous Divine Love that is God within all of us and to see each other as faces of God also.

16

Embracing the Miraculous for Ourselves and the World

(Ramtha) I will love you into knowing God and becoming the unlimitedness that God is (p. 25).
—*Ramtha*, edited by Steven Lee Weinberg

Love is all there is. All there is is Love.
—The Beatles

How can you best embrace and maintain embracing the Miraculous and Optimal Health within yourself? How can you help people worldwide embrace the Miraculous and Attain Optimal Health?

Our body is a microcosm of the whole, so by committing to embrace the Miraculous and attain optimal health, you are creating this on a world level. By dedicating your growth and healing to all your relations worldwide, this prayer manifests itself in people worldwide.

Commitment to live embracing the Universal Energy is the key, and having ongoing support is the way. Are you committed to embracing the miraculous? Are you committed to attaining more energy and health on all levels?

My mission on earth is committing to this for myself and everyone else. In my commitment to help everyone embrace

186

the miraculous and attain optimal health, I have developed ways for you to continue growing. Are you committed to sustaining your energy? Good, applaud yourself and take advantage of my following supports; many are free. Please give a donation if you wish to express your appreciation and want to support more world healing to continue happening in this way. I extend my sincere thanks and gratitude for your donations.

Log onto deepika @holistictherapiesinc.com to receive:

Miraculous Healing Now Web Video Clips

Do you want a free healing? The Universal Love heals the person I am working with, as well as viewers who resonate with any of the issues and healing.

Miraculous Healing Now Ipod Collection

Would you like continuous free healing anywhere, anytime for yourself and everyone you know? These audio healings are added to weekly and categorized by topics. Download all that will benefit you. Promote free world healing to potentially billions of people by telling everyone.

Embracing the Miraculous Meditation Ipod Collection

Do you want to feel more energy? Divinely Loved? Whole? Supported? Healthier? Participate in these free 30-minute mantra meditations. Let others know also.

Embracing Yourself As Miraculous Visualization

Would you like guided visualizations with Divine music to inspire your healing? Use this service and pass it on.

Embracing the Miraculous CD

Do you wish you had music and my voice guiding you through this book's exercises? The first eleven exercises come to life on this CD. Order now!

Order *The Magic Moment* book

How many of you want to live in the magic of the present moment? This book uses fifty-two color photographs and phrases for you to experience living in the present moment while you are sitting, walking and living each moment of your life. Thirty years of sitting meditation helped me to awaken to this experience, which is simplified for you to learn and enjoy not only *The Magic Moment,* but every moment of your life.

Marilyn Laverty, President of Teams on Target, who consults for businesses and facilitates teams with tough decisions, says, *"Deepika has a knack for leading, teaching, writing and healing that has given me profound, life-altering experiences of living in the now, partnering with God and feeling energized, and feeling healthier than ever before for the last fifteen years that I've worked with her. She makes what seems difficult and unreachable readily graspable and simple to live."*

Invest in a *How Healthy Are You? Half-Hour Energetic Assessment*

How healthy are you? I had no symptoms and was climbing 21,000–foot peaks. Hidden radiation and heavy metals nearly killed me a few years later.

The time to prevent disease is before it physically shows up in your body. Prevention costs less in pain, energy, money, and time.

I suggest everyone get biannual energetic body check-ups similar to dental cleanings. I energetically evaluate one hundred and eleven body systems, organs, pathogens, heavy metals, allergies, acid/alkaline ratio, toxicity level, vitamins, minerals, tendencies toward diseases and any other questions within a half-hour. It takes another fifteen minutes to test others in your family including pets.

Invest in a *How Healthy and Energetic Do You Want to Be?*
One-Hour Comprehensive Session

I recommend having the assessment plus the solution. I source the causes of your imbalances physically, mentally, emotionally and spiritually, then give you support with individualized homeopathic remedies, easy to grasp therapeutic homework, Chinese Energetic corrections, and spiritual healing. I guarantee you will feel a healing difference during the session.

"I had long term problems with asthma, high blood pressure, heart, prostate, colon and skin problems. Now I have low blood pressure, and the rest has basically cleared up too. I am breathing better than I have for years." Jim Foster

"Deep-seated anxiety, digestion, elimination problems and chronic fatigue is a thing of my past. Also my thirty-year breast cysts disappeared in three days. I generally feel joyous and energized." Julia

"I was diagnosed with Huntington's disease. Last year people couldn't understand me; I slept most of the day, couldn't walk, was on oxygen around the clock, in the hospital with pneumonia regularly, and unable to eat whole food. Now I am healthy, awake late at night reading scientific articles and writing, eating regular food and going anywhere I wish." Brian

"I had arthritic shoulder pains waking me from sleep, and Renaud's Syndrome—poor finger circulation and numbing. Working with Deepika, these stopped." Michael

Organize Healing Demonstrations or Teleseminar Support Groups

Would you like a great way for you and your friends to receive a healing?

"I received instant healing on all levels in my throat area and tangibly felt the Divine Energy healing my body. It was awesome." Daniel

How many of you want to have more energy and health, as well as **learning** how to do this amazing work yourself? I have a teaching program that trains you to master the Holistic Therapies system that I practice. It begins with two **Embracing the Miraculous You 2-Day Classes and completes with a two-week class.**

Embracing the Miraculous You Two-Day Class

Would you like to deepen your ability to tangibly sense, feel, hear, see, be moved by, and know the Universal Energy, God by any name you choose? Would you like to deepen your trust and ability to follow your guidance? Do you want more clarity about your mission on earth? Would you like to live more of your potential? You will experience all this, plus be introduced to how to heal yourself and others.

One of my students said, *"I found the class with Deepika to be deeply transformative. By aligning myself with Spirit, I learned to stand in a place of integrity and authenticity and now feel blessed in every part of my life. My mission and life have really taken off with Spirit as my partner. Thank you."* Bianca

"When you said, 'Do you feel God?' I felt it. I now trust whatever is going on is okay and for the best. I feel more peace in my life." Marilyn

Embracing the Miraculous You with Love Two-Day Class

Would you like to identify your negative subconscious attitudes and how they are running your life? Would you like to be healthier and happier by transforming your anger, sadness, and fear into unconditional love for yourself and others? Would you like to see yourself from the eyes of God? Are you ready to play and heal?

"I am so grateful to you for my consistently feeling better in every way from the classes and healings. People have been asking me what I am on. All I can say is my awareness of the presence of Divine Love is now always with me. When my vision of the world changed, a whole new world happened to me, and I got my life back." Julia

Embracing the Miraculous Training Program for Healers

How would you like be able to help others instantly heal imbalances on all levels, like chronic disease and gain optimal health on all levels? I share thirty years of my training as a: Naropa University Master's Psychotherapist, Advanced BodyScan/ homeopathist, Chinese Energetics and psychic surgery practitioner in thirteen exciting days, in which you will:

- Learn meditation, become aware of yourself and others energetically, practice living the magic moment and become aligned with the Miraculous, God, by any name, and help others also do this.
- Read and experience all the body systems, organs, minerals, vitamins, pathogens and imbalances.
- Learn basics of the BodyScan and homeopathy to balance the body.
- Learn God psychotherapy and energy readings.
- Learn witnessing Christ doing psychic surgery.

- Learn Yuen Method (Chinese Energetics), reprogramming the meridians and nervous system physically, emotionally, mentally, and spiritually.
- Learn to have Christ and God do group healings
- Learn blood microscope work in proving balances and God's healing.
- Learn to read blood and do microscope work.

"I am so excited to be out of pain and learn a method of healing that really works. I have been an acupuncturist for twenty-five years. In spite of my background, and going to hundreds of healers all my life for my chronic pain, nothing worked until now. I feel liberated. I can help people heal better than ever now using this method combined with my own healing work." Linda

"From the many years I've known Deepika, I've been extremely impressed with her ability to heal herself from a life threatening condition of Grave's disease and heal others from major illnesses. She has done all this from her connection to God. I deeply admire her connection and devotion to God. This is a powerful blessing." Ray Wynfield, healer, minister, teacher of meditation

Embracing the Miraculous Trip to John of God in Brazil Thirteen Days

Do you want to experience one of the most powerful, loving, spiritual healing centers in the world? Do you want a deeper relationship with God/ Universal Love? Do you want deep healing for yourself and the ability to help others more?

May the mission I serve of everyone being aware of their connection with God by all names, Embracing the Infinite Miraculous Love that we are and attaining optimal health or love on all levels be a worldwide reality.

I know this is possible because I have experienced feeling and seeing this infinite love in the Entity's eyes with John of

God serving as the medium. I have physically experienced dying and lived this infinte love for all existence. This is our destiny and it is happening worldwide. Today the Dalai Lama spoke and modeled world love and compassion worldwide via the web. All of us can live love this moment and dedicate our healing "to all our relations" as the American Indians do. God bless all of us to Embrace the Miraculous Love that we are and Attain Optimal Health on All Levels.

Please contact me (Deepika Avanti) and my team by logging onto www.holistictherapiesinc.com, email your requests for sessions, CDs, books, or comments to deepika@holistictherapiesinc.com. Phone 303 440-4431. Mail letters to 698 Dixon Rd., Boulder, CO 80302. Thanks.

Make a World of Difference:
Volunteer to Spread World Healing

If you'd like to be part of Humanity's Team, the global grassroots spiritual movement that is "Awakening the World to our Oneness," please go to www.humanitysteam.org. You will find there many ways to become involved.

If you'd like to help Holistic Therapies create worldwide healing, please email deepika@holistictherapiesinc. I welcome all your help. Thanks, Deepika Avanti

Selected Bibliography

A Course in Miracles, Combined Volume. Tiburon, CA: Foundation for Inner Peace. 1975

Alpert, Richard. Ram Dass. *Still Here. Embracing Aging, Changing, Dying*. New York: Riverhead Books. 2000

Brennan, Barbara. *Light Emerging. The Journey of Personal Healing*. New York, Toronto, London, Sydney, Auckland: Bantam Books. 1993

Borysenko, Joan Ph.D. *Inner Peace for Busy People. 52 Simple Strategies for Transforming Your Life*. Carlsbad, CA., Sydney, Australia: Hay House. 2001

Borysenko, Joan. Dveirin, Gordon. *Saying Yes to Change*. Carlsbad, CA: Hay House. 2006

Bragdon, Emma. *Spiritual Alliances. Discovering the Roots of Health at the Casa de Dom Inacio*. Woodstock, VT: Lightening Up Press. 2002

Brinkley, Dannion with Kathryn Brinkley. *The Secrets of the Light. Spiritual Strategies to Empower Your Life... Here and in the Hereafter*. Henderson, NV: Heart Light Productions. 2004

Brown, Les. Motivational Speaker with Live Full and Die Empty Video DVD, Getting Unstuck

Burley, Philip. *To Master Self Is to Master Life*. Saint Germain Through the Mediumship of Philip Burley. Scottsdale, AZ: Assoc. for Internal Mastery, Inc. 1989

Davis, Audrey Craft. *Making Love with God. The Art of Mental Connection*. Nevada City, CA: Blue Dolphin Publishing. 2006

Chopra, Deepak & Simon, David. *Grow Younger, Live Longer.*
10 Steps to Reverse Aging. New York: Harmony Books.
2001

Chopra, Deepak. *Quantum Healing. Exploring the Frontiers of*
Mind/Body Medicine. New York, Toronto, London, Sydney, Auckland: Bantam Books. 1989

Dyer, Dr. Wayne. *Inspiration: Your Ultimate Calling.* Carlsbad,
CA: Hay House. 2006

Dyer, Dr. Wayne. *Real Magic. Creating Miracles in Everyday Life.*
New York: HarperPaperbacks. 1992

Eker, T. Harv. *Secrets of the Millionaire Mind. Mastering the Inner*
Game of Wealth. New York, NY: HarperBusiness. 2005

Green, Glenda. *Love Without End. Jesus Speaks.* Sedona, Ari-
zona: Spiritis Publishing. 1999

Hay, Louise L. *You Can Heal Your Life.* Santa Monica, CA: Hay
House. 1984

Hendricks, Gay. *Learning to Love Yourself. A Guide to Becoming*
Centered. New York: Simon & Schuster. 1982

Myss, Caroline. *Anatomy of the Spirit. The Seven Stages of Power*
and Healing. New York: Three Rivers Press. 1996

Osteen, Joel. *Your Best Life Now.* New York: Warner Faith.
2004

Peterson, Wayne S. *Extraordinary Times. Extraordinary Beings.*
Experiences of an American Diplomat with Maitreya and
Masters of Wisdom. Charlottesville, VA: Hamptom Roads.
2003

Rael, Joseph. *House of Shattering Light: Life as an American In-*
dian Mystic [Illustrated]. Tulsa, OK: Council Oak Books.
2003

Rajneesh, Bhagwan Shree. *The Book. An Introduction to the*
Teachings of Bhagwan Shree Rajneesh Series II from I to
Q. Rajneeshpuram, OR: Rajneesh Foundation Interna-
tional. 1984

Ramtha. *Ramtha.* Eastsound, WA: Sovereignty, Inc. 1986

Roman, Sanaya. *Living with Joy. Keys to Personal Power, Spiritual Transformation.* Tiburon, CA: H J Kramer Inc., Publishers. 1986

Ruiz, Don Miguel. *The Four Agreements. A Toltec Wisdom Book.* San Rafael, CA: Amber-Allen Publishing. 1997

Saint Germain, medium Burley, Philip. *To Master Self Is to Master Life.* Scottsdale, AZ: Association for Internal Mastery, Inc. 1989

Stibal, Vianna. *Go Up and Work with God.* 2100 Niagara St. Idaho Falls, 83404

Terkeurst, Lysa. *Radically Obedient, Radically Blessed. Experiencing God in Extraordinary Ways*

Yuen, Kam Dr. *Instant Pain Elimination. How to Stop the Pain You Feel in 2 Minutes or Less.* Canoga Park, CA: CEM Publishers. 2003

Yuen, Kam Dr. *Instant Rejuvenation. How to Live to Be Hundred and Not Look or Feel Like a Hundred.*

Yuen, Kam Dr. *The Power of Instant Healing Basic Course.* www.Yuenmethod.com

Walsch, Neale Donald. *Conversations with God: Books 1, 2, 3.* New York: Hampton Roads Publishing. 1996–1998

Walsch, Neale Donald. *Home with God, in a Life That Never Ends.* New York: Atria Books. 2006

Warren, Rick. *The Purpose Driven Life. What on Earth Am I Here For?* Grand Rapids, MI: Zondervan. 2002

Williamson, Marianne. *A Return to Love. Reflections on the Principles of* A Course in Miracles. New York, NY: HarperCollins Publisher, 1992

Major Teachers

Dr. Kam Yuen
and Deepika

Les Brown and Deepika

Joseph Beautiful
Painted Arrow

Harv Ecker and Deepika

*Neale
Donald
Walsh and
Deepika*

My parents

*Nepal, Gokyo Ri
18,500 ft.
son Zen age 6,
Deepika and husband
Charles climbing to
health*

*Peru 19,500 feet, son Zen age 8,
husband Charles age 64,
Deepika age 47*

About the Author

Deepika Avanti, MA, LPC, is a holistic therapist. She received her M.A. from Naropa University and is a licensed psychotherapist, a certified medical intuitive, an advanced, licensed Phazx BodyScan/homeopathic practitioner, certified as a Yuen Method (Chinese Energetic) practitioner, and performs healings through the love and power of Christ. She uses this holistic approach described in this book in her worldwide healing practice, meditation and classes.

Her lifetime quest to tangibly embrace Spirit accelerated when she was told she had an "incurable" disease and discovered "faith," being told she had only three weeks to live. She went from being unable to walk, ninety-five percent dead, to optimal health, climbing 21,000-foot peaks. After healing herself through the various methods described in this book, and finding her answers primarily through relationship with the Miraculous, Love, God by infinite names, she offers this book as a healing tool and inspiration to others.

Deepika is a guide at the Casa in Brazil where the acclaimed healer John of God has worked with millions of people. She also apprenticed with a Ute Indian shaman for seven years, studied many religions and practiced Buddhism over twenty years. This included living in several Ashrams and traveling around the world many times.

Now she lives with her husband, Charles Ogsbury, whose OME banjos are world treasures, and their son, Zen Ogsbury, a master of surprise!

Printed in the United States
201412BV00002B/265-315/P